Praise for *Beating Ana*

"In *Beating Ana*, Shannon Cutts offers a wealth of guidance that will do nothing less than save lives. Shannon has taken her vast experience and condensed it into an intelligent, captivating, and motivating work. This is a book that needs to be in the hands of every person in the eating disorder world: those who suffer, those who love them, and every professional who treats them. I would not stop there . . . the truly amazing beauty of this literary treasure is that it is a book every adult needs to read. As Shannon wisely points out, when it comes to problematic behaviors, 'Everybody has something!' This book can teach us all."

—Doris Smeltzer, M.A., Author of *Andrea's Voice: Silenced by Bulimia,* and the "Advice for Parents" Blog (Gurze Books)

"Unlike any other book about eating disorders, *Beating Ana* uniquely illustrates the importance of people connecting with one another for support and encouragement along the recovery road. I would never have recovered from my own eating disorder without the help of recovered women who held my hand along the way. Shannon's depth of passion and honesty will provide much-needed hope to all those touched by this insidious illness."

—Jenni Schaefer, Author of *Life Without Ed: How One Woman Declared Independence from Her Eating Disorder and How You Can Too*

"*Beating Ana* is a breath of fresh air. Not only is it an important document to add to the record and an item worthy of being in any man or woman's recovery tool bag, but the way in which it is written (engaging, honest, interactive, and fun) guarantees that it'll be a tool that's lovingly worn with repeated use. Recovery often feels like a lonely journey, but thanks to Shannon's innovative approach, the specter of flying solo is no longer a certainty."

—Ron Saxen, Author of *The Good Eater*

"In *Beating Ana*, Shannon takes readers on a journey of self-discovery and self-healing that will leave them truly understanding that recovery *is* possible. I especially liked how each chapter included a "Life Celebration Affirmation" and "Recovery Workshop." These action items engage the reader and compel them to take control of their situation and recover. I highly recommend this book to anyone struggling with an eating disorder, and I plan to use some of the material in my own support groups. I just wish this book was around when I was overcoming my eating disorder—it would have made the process much easier."

—**Andrea Roe, Author of *You Are Not Alone* Volumes I & II (www.youarenotalonebook.com) and Founder of the You Are Not Alone Eating Disorder Society (www.youarenotalonesociety.org)**

"Through Shannon's beautiful prose, she offers her readers honesty, truth, and compassion. She holds a mirror up for us to explore who we are and how we came to be. Shannon provides us with tools for our healing and generously lifts us with her hope. She believes in us. After reading this book, we are left believing in ourselves."

—**Barb Steinberg, LMSW, Workshop Presenter & Consultant (www.barbsteinberg.com)**

"*Beating Ana* has the potential to make a real impact on people dealing with eating disorders, particularly anorexia. The format for this book is unique in the market. I am unaware of any other book on anorexia that uses the format of someone going through the experience and then immediately confronts their thinking with empathy, compassion, and advice learned through having experienced many of the same things. I love that. So often, as I read the letters, I think, *She sounds just like me.* Shannon's responses are always well thought out, helpful, and recovery focused. This book is more like a therapy session that you have written down and can refer back to."

—**Jen L., Anorexia Survivor**

"*Beating Ana* is riveting, compassionate, and remarkable. Shannon brilliantly reveals how individuals can move beyond the grip of their eating disorder to lead an extraordinary and fulfilling existence. Shannon is dynamic and insightful, and each word she writes comes from the heart and soul. She understands the 'Key to Life' that exists within all of us. I would recommend this book as a recovery companion to all those suffering from an eating disorder."

—Lisa C. Palmer, L.M.F.T., C.H.T., Ph.D., The Renew Center of Florida, www.TheRenewCenter.com, MyEDHelp.com, www.MyEDHelp.com

"In *Beating Ana*, I found it easy to feel the love, compassion, and understanding the author has for her mentees and others who struggle with eating disorders. *Beating Ana* helps the reader to truly experience the heart and mind of someone struggling with an eating disorder and gain an accurate measure of understanding and empathy. I felt touched, motivated, and inspired to apply the many lessons taught as well as the heartfelt, practical advice from someone who truly knows the eating disorder recovery process from firsthand experience."

—Lynette L. Taylor, MT-BC, Music Therapist, Center for Change, Inc.

"Mentoring is an ancient and honorable tradition. It brings to mind the relationship with older siblings, trusted community elders, apprentices and master craftspeople, and even traditional spiritual advisors. In *Beating Ana*, Cutts brings experience and compassion to the 'craft' of mentoring and brings it into a field—eating disorders recovery—rich in opportunities to nurture and support each other."

—Laura Collins, Author of *Eating With Your Anorexic*, Founder of F.E.A.S.T.

"*Beating Ana* is a gift! Shannon gets to one of the core problems in eating disorders. Secrecy! This 'secret' leads to shame, isolation, and loneliness. Those struggling with ED feel alone and imprisoned in these vicious lies of the eating disorder. So I strongly agree with Shannon, the way of escape is through mentoring relationships.

Shannon invites us into the sacred places she has walked with her mentees. Through letters you see the real anguish of those tormented by ED. Shannon gently, but powerfully challenges their erroneous beliefs, and becomes a healthy mirror through her Life Celebration Affirmations. Shannon is able to build trust through sharing experiences of her own recovery and therefore offers real hope. Shannon gives practical, relatable 'how to's' through creative journaling exercises, which become a map toward recovery. I would recommend this book to my clients."

—Colleen O'Grady-Long, M.A., L.P.C., L.M.F.T.

Beating ANA

How to Outsmart
Your Eating Disorder &
TAKE YOUR LIFE BACK

Shannon Cutts

Health Communications, Inc.
Deerfield Beach, Florida

www.hcibooks.com

All names found in this book (except as otherwise noted) have been changed to respect privacy. The information contained in this book is based upon the research and personal and professional experiences of the author and reflects the author's professional opinion. The publisher does not advocate the use of any particular healthcare protocol but believes in presenting this information to the public. Should the reader have any questions concerning the appropriateness of any procedures or preparation mentioned herein, the reader should consult a professional healthcare advisor.

The author has no affiliation with the Fellowship of Alcoholics Anonymous or any Twelve Step-based organization.

Permissions

The excerpts from A.A. material are reprinted with permission of Alcoholics Anonymous World Services, Inc. ("AAWS") Permission to reprint these excerpts does not mean that AAWS has reviewed or approved the contents of this publication, or that AAWS necessarily agrees with the views expressed herein. A.A. is a program of recovery from alcoholism only—use of these excerpts in connection with programs and activities which are patterned after A.A., but which address other problems, or in any other non A.A. context, does not imply otherwise.

The excerpt from *On Death & Dying* is reprinted with permission of Scribner, a division of Simon & Schuster Adult Publishing Group, from ON DEATH & DYING by Elisabeth Kubler-Ross. Copyright © 1997 by Elisabeth Kubler-Ross. All rights reserved.

Library of Congress Cataloging-in-Publication Data

Cutts, Shannon.

Beating ANA : how to outsmart your eating disorder and take your life back / Shannon Cutts

p. cm.

ISBN-13: 978-0-7573-1385-1 (trade paper)

ISBN-10: 0-7573-1385-X (trade paper)

1. Eating disorders—Popular works. I. Title.

RC552.E18C88 2009

616.85'26—d22   2008049566

Publisher: Health Communications, Inc.
3201 S.W. 15th Street
Deerfield Beach, FL 33442–8190

Cover photos ©Mehmet Salih Guler, iStockphoto
Cover design by Larissa Hise Henoch
Interior design and formatting by Lawna Patterson Oldfield

For every person who has—
even for a second—
lost hope that recovery
really *is* possible.

This book is for you.

If I don't make some significant changes, this is not all going to "turn out okay," is it, Shannon? Yikes. Lots to think about, but thinking can be a waste of time when you don't follow it with doing! *If it weren't for food, everything would be just* fine! *Kidding, kidding!*

—Nadia

You are good at whatever you choose to do with your life, Nadia. If you choose to die, you will be very good at dying. If you choose to live—well, guess what—you will find that you are equally good at saving your own life. Just shift your awareness and intention daily toward living; swing the loaded cannon of all that misdirected potential around, point it at your eating disorder, and fire away.

—Shannon

Contents

Part Two: **ED, A.A., and Me**

Part Three: **ED at the Movies**

Part Four: ED on My Mind

"For Now Let Me Just Say (a poem for the fighter in all of us)"

Sometimes I feel like I have more to say to myself
But I can't find the words. And all that comes to mind is—

I am beautiful.
I am worthy of living
and loving.
I am exquisite—unique.
I am believable—as me.

Why did I waste all these years . . . ?!?

Never mind. Ignore her.
I'm back. I am grateful.
The eating disorder, the depression, the anxiety—
they were all just signposts.
They were my South, East, and West
pointing me North to NOW.

Now . . . when I know I am beautiful.
Now . . . when I know I am worthy of living
and loving.
Now . . . when I know I am exquisite—unique.
Now . . . when I know I am beautiful—as me.
Now . . . when I know that, YES, I am capable of achieving great things

But, more importantly, I know that I have already achieved great things because—

I survived.
I survived myself.
I survived others' pain.
I survived this media-saturated society we live in
with body, mind, heart, and soul stubbornly
intact.

In fact, I did more than survive.
I regrouped.
I restored.
I rebuilt.
I revived.

And even now I am regrouping.
I am restoring.
I am rebuilding.
I am reviving, discovering, accepting, and exploring
the "me" in all this.
The me who got lost and left behind.
The me who was forgotten and misplaced her voice
for a while because of it.

So amazing—she sings again.

I sing again.

And I speak.

I speak out against some

But mostly toward all of us

Who have splintered off our hearts and souls

from our minds and bodies . . .

who have forgotten that we are all whole by design

and that whole is the only way.

Whole is beautiful.

Whole is worth living

and loving.

Whole is exquisite—utterly unique.

Whole is believable—the only believable you and me.

And most of all, whole is the only thing worth dying,

living, and fighting for . . . do we ever really realize—

You are the only you who ever was, is, or ever will be.

And I am the only me.

Sometimes I feel like I have more to say to myself—to everyone—

But I just can't find the words.

So for now, let me just say—

TRUST. HOPE. FAITH. LOVE. LIVE. **TRIUMPH.** BELIEVE.

Foreword:
How to Save a Life

I didn't know that when I answered the phone and spoke for the first time to Shannon Cutts that so many lives would be saved. I was just doing what I do, being an advocate for women's voices in recovery and mentoring (when I could) up-and-coming writers, speakers, and survivors of eating disorders.

Shannon had a story that so many have. Anorexia and bulimia threatened to take her life and disempowered her from enjoying a healthy freedom. But Shannon was less interested in wallowing in her story of struggling with an eating disorder and more interested in beating it. She was more interested in learning to take the harsh and dangerous lessons her eating disorder had bestowed upon her and turning them into a mission, a crusade, and a message that it's not what happens to us that matters, but what we do with what happens to us that is a measure of someone's life.

Beating ANA is a fine and beautiful testament to the power and strength each of us has to first achieve recovery from eating disorders and then parlay our own victory into helping others find their freedom from this disease. Shannon introduces us to six brave women who have courageously battled their obsession with body, weight, and food. They fought against expensive and often limiting recovery systems and found an incredible value in sharing their stories with others, using multiple modalities for healing, and most of all, found the deep strength not to give up.

As an eighteen-year survivor of EDNOS (Eating Disorders Not Otherwise Specified) I can tell you firsthand that relapsing is a normal part of recovery—one must take a few steps back to take many steps forward. Oftentimes the biggest variable in whether people truly recover from an eating disorder is the community of support that is set up to help in their recovery. High recidivism rates occur when people go back into their community following in-patient treatment and find that they may have a few new tools to use against their disease, but the tools pale in comparison to the overwhelming existing structures and triggers that already occur in their everyday lives.

Shannon has crafted a structure to this book that I find immensely helpful: "The Mentor Model." The Mentor Model approach outlines uniquely practical and highly effective recovery tools and techniques that can complement any existing treatment program. Eating disorders thrive in isolation, secrecy, and shame. To recover, we need to break through the isolation, break open the secrecy, and break up the shame—and we cannot do that alone. For lasting recovery to occur, we need each other. In the Mentor Model outlined in *Beating ANA*, Shannon clearly shows us how "relationships replace eating disorders."

The overall structure to this book speaks more to the general call to action Shannon is creating—she wants you to be, in her words, "one more." One more person who survives. One more person who learns to thrive in the face of overwhelming odds. One more person who uses the story of their eating disorder as a catalyst for change and growth in someone else's life.

I have spoken about eating disorders to women from Sri Lanka to Sacramento and they all share one thing in common. They long to recover fully and move on to live a life of purpose. What we fail to remember sometimes is that eating disorders tend to impact the bright, sensitive, and visionary people of our time. Our propensity toward service turns into people-pleasing and other codependent functions that feed eating-disordered thinking. That's why it is important that *Beating ANA* satisfies the step-by-step approach that the mind craves while helping the reader create the supportive community that a heart and soul requires to maintain recovery success.

Gandhi said, "You must be the change you wish to see in the world," and Shannon Cutts has created a written version of the change she wishes to see. From the first moment I spoke with her, it was clear she was a warrior for the cause, a young woman who was not going to let her eating disorder become her identity. In fact, she has gone on to leave a different legacy by reaching a hand out to other women and encouraging them to find their own strength and then pay it forward. For those of us who long to see a world where not another eight-year-old counts calories and not another forty-year-old hides her childhood secrets through bingeing, then we must all do our part to become educated and then empowered to make a difference. By picking up this book, proactively practicing the techniques in each chapter, seeking out mentors in your own community, and in time becoming a mentor yourself to someone in need, you are doing your part. You are being your own agent for change, and the ripple effect is incalculably precious and powerful not just in your own life, but in the lives of those who come behind you and seek to follow your example.

Shannon Cutts's *Beating ANA* will not only move you, it will become a necessary inspiration in your life and help you realize that you can indeed rewrite your own story of recovery from an eating disorder. You'll be in awe of the six women featured in these pages, who have so generously shared their sometimes messy, often halting, but always fruitful and productive recovery stories to support and encourage you. But most of all you will be in awe to learn you are just like them and that you do indeed have what it takes to save a life. First, your own, then another's.

With love and light,

Jessica Weiner

Author of *A Very Hungry Girl* and *Life Doesn't Begin 5 Pounds From Now*

Acknowledgments

For most authors, writing a book is a solo effort. However, I think it is safe to say that, for all authors, editing and actually publishing a book takes a *team*.

My team is simply amazing. Wonderful. Phenomenal. Going above and beyond, again and again. I suspect they have superpowers they don't tell me about because they don't want me to get jealous (too late). They have beautiful minds, hearts, and spirits. They are a more than generous gift to one lone writer with a dream to share her own experiences of hope, healing, and recovery with the world. Who knew when I tattooed the symbol for "wisdom" on my foot that such an *army* of wise advisors would appear?!?

To Annie and Lynn, my mentors. Where would I be without you today? No place I want to know about! You have my gratitude, and my heart.

To Richard Cholakian of RGC Entertainment, my longtime manager and booking agent. You told me you would, and you have "shown me how it's done"—The RGC Way. I am suitably honored ... humbled ... grateful ... and seriously impressed!

To Laura Collins, my tireless writing mentor and friend. 250 perfectly good pages lost their lives when I met you. My book, and my life, is the better for it.

To Doris Smeltzer, who by her own example, encouragement, validation, and gentle guidance, paved the way for refinements in this manuscript that have made all the difference.

To Laurie Harper of Sebastian Agency, my "guardian literary agent." Who knew getting a book published could feel like flying?

To Michele Matrisciani of Health Communications, Inc., my "guardian editor." You are the "better half" of this book. My book thanks you, its readers thank you, and, most of all, I thank you.

To the HCI team, who banded together to turn this project around in (literally!) record time—what else can I say but *wow*.

To Nadia, Michelle, Jenna, Krista, and Lori, whose voices and stories bring the pain, and the triumphant joy, of recovery to life.

To Jess Weiner, who has supported me and believed in me since the idea for this book was first conceived. You knew I could do it before I did, which is just one of the many reasons why it is such an honor to share your voice in these pages now.

To Robin Richardson, who has courageously walked similar steps to my own and emerged to validate the process, the program, and the path for us both. I am moved by your support, encouragement, and enthusiasm for sharing this work, in these pages and far beyond.

To Andrea Roe, friend, fellow survivor, and founding member, along with Lynn and Robin, of *Mentor*CONNECT—your enthusiasm, dedication, poise, and courage inspire my own.

To Monica Lane, aka "Gayle." You've got the job, girl!

To M. D. Thompson of the Ivory Tower, who has always made sure that the music I write to support this work sings in perfect harmony with my words.

To Jenni Schaefer, for being such a light of encouragement.

To John and Alicia Nash. Thank you for sharing your beautiful story and illumining the path for us all.

To all those who suffer from eating and related disorders who have written to me through the years to share your stories of recovery, encourage me in my work, and then *join* me by serving as a mentor to those who need you—*thank you*.

To those who work in the field of eating disorders recovery, and especially to each of my wonderful advance readers who have welcomed me so warmly into your world. Your words, and your work, make all the difference.

And to each of *you*, the readers, who, just by holding this book in your hands, share in the dream of our chance, and right, to one day live in a world *free* from eating disorders!

To "The Fam." We have learned and grown so much together over the years. An eating disorder truly is a "family affair"—thank you so much for the respect, love, and generosity you have shown me by supporting me as I share our story.

To Eli, for reminding me of the simple joys of being little. And to Adam and Erin, his generous parents, who in their love for each other also gifted me with an adorable nephew!

To Kerry (bfffffffffffffffffff!!!!). Nuff said. You rock, girl.

To the "urban tribe" . . . you know who you are. YouTube, the revolutionary iPhone, Santa Pub Crawl, hurricane parties, the worst song in the world, Red Robin and a flick for the 40th (or is it 400th) time, through breakups, weddings, births, deaths, music CDs, and the writing of one small book . . . you have always been there for me. Yo yo, dawg. Dial Idol. Today.

To all the countless friends and peers who have supported, encouraged, and cheered me on over the years . . . so little time, so many amazing encouragers, in so many wonderful ways. Remember—to the world you may be just one person, but to that one person you may mean the world! So now you know.

To David Black, my friend and webmaster. I miss you. You are irreplaceable. RIP 4-18-08.

To Pearl, aka "love with wings." The most beautiful cockatiel in the world, and don't you know it. You taught me what beauty looks and acts like (although I certainly hope it doesn't screech like that).

And last and smallest . . . to Gill, III, and Bob, IV, my blue and red betta fish. Every time I was tempted to take me, my life, or my writing too seriously, you would start to chase your tails. In those moments, you gotta ask yourself, *Who can stay serious with a blue betta who thinks he's a puppy?*

Until next time, all. Same time, same place, next book?

Warmly, with love and—always—with HOPE,

Shannon

Preface

This book offers you a taste of pure human goodness—help and hope being offered without a hook, catch, or high price tag. It reminds us of the big life questions: Why are we here? What is our purpose? Shannon suggests that our highest purpose is to be useful to others and to be connected to each other in a chain of human caring—one hand reaching forward for help, one hand reaching back to lend assistance. For Shannon, the miracle of recovering her life from an eating disorder gives her a unique ability and calling to reach back and help those who are still struggling, just as she stays connected to and leans upon those who have gone before her on this healing journey.

Like Shannon, I am recovering from an eating disorder that started in my early adolescence. And, like Shannon, I owe my life to being mentored. The mentoring that I received—much of which I experienced through the Twelve Steps of recovery—came from other women who were recovering. I accepted their help because it was free and I was desperate, alone, and out of hope. Even more important, I was willing to trust these women because they made two things clear to me—they knew intimately the hell I was living in, and they believed that I too could get out. They were my companions and guides as I slowly climbed the ladder up and out of a life consumed with disordered eating.

Now as a therapist, singer/songwriter, and public speaker on the topic of eating disorders, I agree with Shannon that there is no better use of a life than to give hope and to inspire others to recover. Much of my own recovery has been strengthened through helping others who are struggling with disordered eating. Being able to use my own painful experiences to benefit others has been the most remarkable and transcendent gift of my own life. I know, as does Shannon, that nothing is too big, dark, or difficult to recover from.

Shannon describes eating disorders as having the ability to outlast our financial, emotional, and familial resources. In order to heal, we need all the help that we can possibly gather from therapists, doctors, nutritionists, psychiatrists, family, friends, and so on—in essence the "support team." Shannon suggests the addition of a mentor to this team—defining "mentor" as one who is recovering and one who understands and can give hope and support from an insider's perspective. I believe this is a crucial missing piece in the recovery process—one that could especially help those who are either unable to receive treatment or who simply need additional support during or after treatment. It is essential that the members of the support team work together, joining their energies and embracing all of the different and valuable aspects of recovery provided by each member of the team. Mentors are *not* to be seen as a substitute or replacement for professional help, but rather as an addition to the support team.

Shannon states emphatically that "relationships replace eating disorders." I couldn't agree more, as I know my own disordered eating behaviors were a desperate attempt to fill a deep longing for connection. Shannon envisions a mentor-mentee relationship as a healthy relationship to fill the gaps between individual and group therapy sessions, lend a helping hand for tackling daily life situations and struggles, and model healthy recovery behaviors. Most importantly, a mentor would consistently give *hope*—the kind of hope that only someone who has first conquered a significant recovery-related issue in their own lives can give. This book shows how mentoring works, as Shannon shares letters from her mentees and her responses, as mentor, back to them.

I am humbled and filled with gratitude for Shannon's generosity, dedication to helping others recover, and the strength of her spirit. This book is her gift—a wise and empathetic hand to hold for those needing a guiding light to lead them out of the hell of disordered eating. She offers wisdom in specific stepping-stones or exercises, called "Recovery Workshops," that marked important stages in her own journey. No matter where you are in your recovery process, this book will help strengthen your commitment to life and support you in finding and celebrating your own unique and unrepeatable beauty.

—*Robin Richardson, MA, CMT*

Part One

WELCOME TO OUR WORLD

Making the transition from being one of the many who suffers from an eating disorder (ED) to becoming one of the few who triumphs over your eating disorder is as rocky as any I can think of. Quite possibly, the only experience tougher on a human body, mind, heart, and spirit than falling ill is getting better.

It gets unnecessarily tougher, however, when we assume that we will have to heal the same way we got sick—alone. We don't. In fact, I couldn't. My loneliness and isolation were precisely the reasons why recovery felt so difficult—impossible, really. So here, in this first section,

I will introduce you to a whole new approach to eating
disorders recovery—an approach that worked for me
when I had literally lost all hope of surviving my eating
disorder in any other way—an approach that has the very
same power to renew your hope and transform your
experience of recovery.

So what are we waiting for? Let's get started!

❧ ❧ ❧

It is our Tuesday evening support group. On tiptoes,
speaking in hushed whispers, they sidle forward, eyes
groundward, chests barely rising and falling, curling up
into the depths or balancing on the edges of their chosen
seats. . . . They are afraid to breathe too loudly for fear
someone will notice.

It is scary to be noticed when you don't like what
you've become. It is scarier still to be noticed when you
don't know who you are. And when the little you do know
of yourself consists of the constant competition, comparison, and criticism of an eating disorder in your head, at
first it can be very scary to be noticed keeping company
with others like you . . . to realize that you, and your eating
disorder, are *not alone*.

But eventually, if you want to heal, if you want to live,
you adjust. You get used to two things—one, being
noticed, and two, not being the only one with an eating
disorder. You also get used to not being the only one with
depression, anxiety, panic attacks, obsessive-compulsive

disorder, low self-esteem, self-harm, promiscuity or sexual anorexia, substance abuse, alcoholism, borderline personality disorder, post-traumatic stress disorder, bottomless fear, uncontrollable anger, and endless aching loneliness . . . and you get used to sharing the burden of guilt generated by being willing, for quite some time now, to do just about anything and everything to ease the void within, even if what you are driven to do drags you down, and then drags everyone else down with you. In fact, oddly enough, this sense of collective ownership is eventually part of what gives you some small, and, in time, much greater relief.

This process—of harnessing the transformative, healing, relieving power of naming, owning, and then *sharing* both the pain and the promise of recovery with at least one other person who has been there, understands, and is willing and able to help—is called mentoring. Mentoring neatly circumvents the isolation in which an eating disorder flourishes by putting us in direct connection with each other—heart to heart, mind to mind, spirit to spirit. Mentoring has become a virtually lost art in this isolating age of eating disorders. Yet I have spent the past twenty years of my life putting into daily practice, and the last five years compiling, the material you hold in your hands now, because mentoring *saved my life*. I have seen it save the lives of many of my mentees, and I believe it has the same power to save your life as well.

It is also worth mentioning that many different names exist for what I call mentoring. For instance, we will discuss a bit later how the success of the worldwide fellowship of Alcoholics Anonymous is structured around the art and discipline of sponsorship. Similarly, many outreach organizations offer the chance to seek out a "Big Brother" or "Big Sister" to share life's challenges and victories. It is often possible to form similar bonds within the context of an ongoing therapeutic relationship as well. Here, I introduce my own highly successful experiences of first being mentored, and now mentoring others, through what I call "The Mentor Model." This model, which we will explore in much greater depth shortly, will serve as our guide as we unfold the full potential and promise that a mentoring relationship holds for you in your journey to meet—and even exceed!—your recovery goals.

Why have I dedicated countless hours of my personal time to serve as a mentor and five years of my life to write this book? For one simple reason—because mentoring takes us back to the heart of what it means to be human, which is that we need each other or we will not, cannot, survive. My own battle to survive my eating disorder took an undeniable, almost unbelievable turn for the better with the appearance of one single, willing, able human being— my own mentor. She was all I had—the only source of help and support I had access to when I was ill and trying to get better—and mysteriously, miraculously, it was enough.

Before we proceed further, I want to make it clear that, regardless of my particular circumstances during my recovery journey, I am not now, nor will I ever be, an advocate of *choosing* to "go it alone"—even with your mentor by your side. Rather, our consistent focus here will be an exploration of the many reasons why it is of value to consider *adding* a mentor to any existing professional support network you have in place. However, over the years I continue to meet many people who, for one reason or another, are confronting the challenge of overcoming their eating disorder without having access to professional medical care, just as I experienced when I was sick. If you are one of these people, holding this book in your hands right now, and you are considering throwing in the towel, then know this—regardless of the circumstances in which you find yourself, regardless of the level of care you currently have access to, regardless of what you think your options are or your prognosis is or can be, you must simply set your mind and heart and spirit to do *whatever it takes* to get better and *never ever give up*.

Hopefully, even as you are reading this now, you have a full treatment team encircling you with all of the care, support, expertise, love, compassion, and guidance you could ever need to heal. But whether you do or do not, there is absolutely no reason to allow yourself to think that you cannot, somehow, some way, no matter what obstacles appear to stand between you and your recovery goals, get better—my own story is living proof of this! Against all odds, with the help of just one caring person who was willing to serve as my mentor when I needed her, I *survived* a devastating fifteen-year battle with anorexia and bulimia . . . and have been in sustained recovery for over a decade now!

Let me say this one more time, that in my own direct, personal experience, there is never, ever, *ever* any reason to give up *hope*. You can do better than that. You *must* do better than that. This world needs you. You are here for a reason. You *matter*. You were always meant to, designed to, and able to survive whatever life hands you and come out ahead, flying the flag of victory! No matter what your situation is, there is always something more you can do to save your own life. There is always more help available to you than first meets the eye. If I could do it—if I could find a way to heal, and *stay* healed, when absolutely no way seemed to exist in my life as I knew it in those days, then *you can too*.

Here is the secret to your success, the secret I learned during the years I spent working toward my own success-ful recovery, and the powerful secret I now pass along to you. Through the years when I was doing the bulk of my recovery work, and in the years since then, it has been and continues to be my experience today that even with all that we now know about eating disorders that we did not know then, and even with all of the resources we have now that I did not have when I first became ill, our most powerful resource for healing, survival, and revival of life continues to be *each other*. Today, even as the work I do at times takes me into some complicated territory, the credo I live by remains simple, direct, profound.

Relationships replace eating disorders. Period. The end.

This is my life's work. This is who I am. This is how I live—and stay alive.

And what a wonderful, worthwhile life it is! Today, post-recovery, I am privileged to spend my days working one-on-one with those in recovery from eating disorders and those who love them, speaking and singing across the country through my outreach organization *Key to Life: unlocking the door to hope,* writing this book and monthly columns for several recovery organizations, and recording music inspired by all of the courageous fighters I meet along the way. All of these endeavors are structured with mentoring in mind, and in such a way as to purposefully demystify what author Peggy Claude-Pierre terms "the secret language of eating disorders," so that those who have no voice can borrow mine until they reclaim their own, and those in a position to help can clearly hear and understand the unspoken and unspeakable need, and move quickly to lend their aid.

That is the purpose for this book—to give to you what I was given from my mentor—*hope*—and through this gift to awaken within you your own ability to *fight* for your life.

That is the purpose of my life—to offer you living, breathing proof that recovery lies within your reach also, and to light the way so that you too can experience for yourself the incredible triumph of *Beating ANA* once and for all!

There is, quite simply, no better use of a life—at least not that I can think of. There is no other life that I would choose than this one—every single heart-wrenching, heart-warming day of it. I will admit I often wasn't sure at the time I was struggling to heal, but today I know that it was all worth it—the years of struggling, of not knowing, of feeling so scared, and then to see the sun begin to come up over the horizon and to realize that *I am doing it* . . . that thing I thought *I could not do* . . . and then realizing that if *I* could do it, then *so can you* . . . WOW.

Talk about a life worth living—a life worth saving, a life worth surviving for. Today, for me, that life that is so worth living, saving, and surviving for is mine—*and your own*.

My Story

When I first got sick with anorexia, at the age of eleven, no one talked about eating disorders—to me or anyone else. I had been molested by a neighborhood man at the age of six, which created an innate distrust of my surroundings, not to mention a sensitivity to the senseless nature of personal physical and emotional violation that would stay with me from that point forward.

By age thirteen, peer cruelty and family turmoil had left their additional marks, and yet I spent the first seven years of my battle with anorexia harboring absolutely no suspicions that my problems were caused by anything other than "just me, being me." My family appeared to feel similarly. We simply didn't know any better, and neither did anyone around us. I continued to decline, year after year, and everyone close to me fell away, as mystified as I was by my slow descent, and unable and uninvited to venture into the intimate, secret places where only the eating disorder and I could go.

When I turned eighteen, I left my family and moved to another state to attend university. I was already a nationally recognized up-and-coming young jazz and bluegrass musician, and I had been accepted to a prestigious music program. Unfortunately, my "best friend," the eating disorder, had no useful advice for me to help me cope with the stresses and strains of a whole new life, let alone the demands that my college's music department directors placed on me. Before too long my physical and mental health caved in. Not even three months into my freshman year, my parents arrived to pack up my things.

I dropped out of school and flew home. Not knowing where else to turn, I found myself crawling even deeper inside my eating disorder for comfort. I couldn't face my family, my few remaining friends, or the cold, hard facts of such an abrupt end to such a promising music career, let alone the heavy weight of guilt I felt for somehow letting it happen. Like an athlete, over time my patterns of overpracticing and persistent, consistent weight loss had steadily weakened my body, including the ligaments and tendons I had relied on to maintain my ten-hour-per-day practice regimen. The doctors told my parents they had never seen such a severe performance injury in one so young—that my injuries resembled those of a thirty-year-career musician. They told me I had better proceed to Plan B, but I had no Plan B. I had no sense of "me" without music. All I had left of the person I had previously referred to as "me" were hard casts on both hands and forearms . . . indefinitely. I couldn't even lift a milk carton or turn a doorknob, let alone engage in the sole form of expression that had offered me a safe way to "speak" the words and emotions that now remained bottled up inside, hour after hour, day after day. I was in constant, ever-deepening pain, both inside and out. Worst of all, I remained in ignorance of the name of my tormentor. I still labored under the assumption that the total collapse of my life was "just me, being me." I wrote myself off, and miserably, unbearably, inconceivably settled down to die.

Meanwhile, my mother searched around and found a physical therapist for me to try and at least salvage my musical dreams. Mom drove me to her office once a week, sometimes twice if things got really bad. My new therapist's name was Annie. I liked her well enough, although I never said much during our initial sessions together, other than politely asking for the occasional clarification of her instructions for the physical therapy exercises she assigned. Privately I thought that she seemed like a strong, happy, confident woman—someone I felt quite sure I could never find anything in common with.

One day, a few months after we started working together, I arrived at her office not just quiet and reserved, but mute and silent. She sat me down, very gently, and said, "Today we will not do physical therapy. Today, we will just talk." She explained that she knew I needed someone to talk to, that she could see I was hurting. Furthermore, she told me she believed that if I didn't talk to someone soon, I might actually explode from the strain of holding it all in, whatever it was, that was pushing so desperately against my seams to get out. I opened my mouth, intending to quickly thank her for her concern, and to assure her that all was well and there was no need to worry. I opened my mouth . . . and it all came flooding out.

The depth of relief I felt was incalculable, mind-blowing, and instantaneous. After seven long years of battling my disease in lonely silence, after I had long since given up hope of help ever arriving, Annie *noticed* my pain. Even more miraculous, she seemed to understand what that unnameable pain inside me felt like from personal experience. She also appeared to possess the ability to do what I could not—separate the particular issue that was causing such a struggle from the human being underneath who was struggling. She saw *me* . . . trapped inside, held down by the weight of my disease, but still alive and willing to fight and wanting to survive. She heard *me* . . . my nearly inaudible actual voice, crying out for recognition beneath the eating disorder voice's vicious lies. She cared about *me* . . . in a way I had never even considered caring about myself.

She wasn't at all intimidated by my pain or my disease or my shame, or even my inability to put any of it into comprehensible words at first, because in her own way she had walked through those same places in her life and had emerged whole and healthy and strong. She also—amazingly, unbelievably—seemed to believe in me, even when it felt impossible to believe in myself, and even while I faltered and fell so many times that her continued presence and support seemed less like compassion and more like insanity.

It was only later that I learned that the reason she was able to do this for me was because someone else had first believed in her and stood by her when she needed that person most.

Annie was my first mentor. She was my first anything—the first person I had ever met who proved to me that an ordinary person like me could be a hero in her own life. She taught me this by showing me, through her own example, that everybody has "something"—something that we each struggle with, something that life hands us, individually, which forces us to wake up and choose life every day, in every way, in every thought, word, and action, because choosing anything less than life means we will not survive, and what a waste of a perfectly wonderful, irreplaceable, unrepeatable life that would be!

Annie also taught me that this "something"—*my* something— meant not that I was weak, but that I was *human*. It meant that I was not to be forcibly, willingly even, separated from the herd of humanity all around me by the perceived unusual weakness within me, but rather that this very challenge I was facing was what *included* me and made me very much *like* the surrounding herd. Annie shared with me something I would never have realized on my own—that, in struggling through my particular "something," I was simply participating with each person around me in the normal and necessary rites of passage life offers us. In other words, I was having my own individual experience of the collective "human condition." Most importantly, I learned from Annie that it was only when we all come together to share in both the burdens and blessings that life offers to us that we each activate our inner power to fully live.

This insight did more to bolster my courage for the journey ahead than any other single "aha" moment during my recovery journey, because in the first instant I understood the true meaning of Annie's words, I received permission and the right to *rejoin* the rest of humanity—to once again occupy my rightful, reserved space to share the pain and the poignancy, the power and the personal responsibility we each bear for uplifting us all, one life at a time.

As we will discuss in more detail in parts three and four, John Nash may have explained this process best when, in the movie about his life, *A Beautiful Mind*, he outlines his Nobel Prize–winning discovery, the Nash Equilibrium. Previously, in economic circles, it had long been assumed that the good of the individual was achieved by each individual looking out for his or her own needs, with no thought or care for how their choices or opportunities might affect the group. Nash discovered that, in fact, the exact opposite was true. The good of the individual can only be achieved when the individual seeks both his or her own good *and the good of the group.*

This is mentoring in a nutshell, and these are words to live by.

Words *I* live by.

Words *you* can live by, survive by, thrive by too.

This is why I have come to meet you here—so that I can say to you with pride, humility, and the unshakeable conviction that if I could heal from my eating disorder, *anyone* who wants to heal badly enough *and is willing to do the hard work of recovery* can do so too.

And maybe, just maybe, through these pages, your eyes will be opened to someone in your life who is willing and able to mentor you, as Annie mentored me. This is my wish for you—to have courage, to let support in wherever it may be found, and to use it to *overcome*.

I was mentored. I became a mentor myself. Now, I pass it on to you.

Welcome to our world—the world of overcomers, survivors, and thrivers. We are so glad you are here!

Shannon

The Mentor Model
(aka Relationships Replace Eating Disorders)

W hy is it that a mentoring relationship can serve as such a powerful catalyst for positive change in recovery? For that matter, why add a mentor to an already full plate of recovery work?

Relationships replace eating disorders. Period. The end. The more loving, supportive, therapeutic relationships that exist in your life, the more the odds of recovery shift in favor of a return to health.

So then, what is the "Mentor Model"? To answer that, let us first define terms. For our purposes here, a "mentor" is a trusted guide who has knowledge and experience in a certain area, and is willing and able to share it. A "mentee" is a person in need of guidance and instruction, and is willing to receive it. Thus, the Mentor Model is simply the voluntary, ongoing, interactive relationship between mentor and mentee (giver and receiver), for the sole purpose of facilitating progress in recovery.

You do not need to have been suffering for a certain length of time, nor do you need to have reached a certain degree of physical or mental ill health, to be mentored and have the process work for you. You will know you are ready to consider adding a mentor to your support team when you can honestly realize and admit that your efforts on your own, if you do not have access to professional medical care, or in concert with your current treatment plan and support system, are not yet getting you to where you want to go with your recovery goals. And, just as I did when the offer of support came to me and I accepted, I am confident that you will know when you are ready and willing to receive what a mentor has to offer.

Ultimately, being mentored can be one of the most profoundly loving, healing, empowering, and life-transforming relationships you will ever encounter. Similarly, serving as a mentor, when the time is right and you are ready, can be tremendously strengthening and confirming for your own continued recovery.

The Alcoholics Anonymous Factor

Our recovery is based on sharing our experience, strength and hope with each other, that we may solve our common problem; more importantly, our continued sobriety depends upon helping others to recover from alcoholism.

— Alcoholics Anonymous (from the A.A. Fact Sheet)

In the world of eating disorders, the concept of pairing a more experienced guide with a newcomer in recovery is still largely relegated to the sidelines. The role of the mentor is all too often overlooked.

But there is another arena where a similar partnership is enthusiastically accepted, endorsed, and effective—and has been since 1935.* In the worldwide fellowship of Alcoholics Anonymous (A.A.), the foundation for achieving lasting sobriety is built when a trusted guide, the "sponsor," guides a newcomer, the "sponsee," to recovery through working the Twelve Steps (see additional resources).

I have a close friend, Lynn, who is not only recovering from an eating disorder but is also in strong recovery from the disease of alcoholism. She credits this recovery to her longtime membership in A.A. and her work with her own sponsor. Several years ago, as I continued in my recovery work to heal from my eating disorder, I noticed that while I had largely overcome my disordered eating behaviors, I was instead beginning to use alcohol and relationships to manage life issues that still felt overwhelming. At that point, Lynn began working with me as both sponsor and mentor, blending together basic recovery principles from the Twelve Steps with troubleshooting sessions to handle my daily life challenges.

Although I had been engaged in mentoring those with eating disorders prior to this point, it was through my work with Lynn that I began to see the truly exciting potential the Mentor Model holds. I found certain concepts from the Twelve Steps particularly helpful in framing pivotal recovery decisions I needed to make. And our daily troubleshooting sessions ensured that once I had made those

---

*In 1960, a Twelve Step–based program called Overeaters Anonymous (O.A.) was founded to assist those who identify themselves as being "powerless over food." In 2000, a second complementary fellowship, Eating Disorders Anonymous (EDA) was founded by A.A. members in Phoenix, AZ.

decisions I then had the support and skills to remain steady on the path. In short, I began to experience for myself how a relationship that has worked so well for those recovering from alcoholism could be equally effective in facilitating recovery from eating disorders.

There are many approaches that hold promise for strengthening our ability to recover. In the beginning, middle, and end, it really all boils down to this: When we all work together—doctor, therapist, nutritionist, psychologist, psychiatrist, social worker, family, friend, sponsor, and mentor—in the name of saving a life, we cannot help but to expect and experience brilliant results.

The A.A. Cooperation with the Professional Community Committee (CPC) . . . informs professionals and future professionals about A.A.—what we are, where we are, what we can do, and what we cannot do. They attempt to establish better communication between A.A.'s and professionals, and to find simple, effective ways of cooperating without affiliating.

—Alcoholics Anonymous Conference-Approved Literature

How This Book Will Work Best

In the years since I began serving as a mentor, I have received literally thousands of e-mails and letters from people all over the world who are seeking help and support to achieve freedom from their eating disorder. Each letter I read is special, unique, moving—a fragment of the full story of the person who wrote it. With some, our exchange is brief—one letter, one response is enough to meet their need at that moment. With others, a second, third, fourth letter soon follows the first . . . creating over time a deep and lasting bond between us.

Often I correspond with several mentees at one time, and this gift has allowed me to begin to recognize common themes in our correspondence—certain questions, fears, obstacles, myths, misconceptions, stumbling blocks, and opportunities that each mentee seems to encounter at some point along the recovery path. One day, it occurred to me that if my particular group of mentees consistently struggles to overcome similar issues, then the chances are good that these are issues common to most who enter into the process of achieving recovery from an eating disorder.

Over time, I have also realized that I can no longer serve as a mentor to each person who writes to me—I am just one person, and a mentoring relationship often requires a significant time commitment to prove fruitful to the mentee. Yet I could not help but continue to dream of finding a way to offer personalized mentoring to each person who wanted it.

To this end, five of my longtime dedicated and courageous mentees have generously "donated" our past correspondence for this book so that you too can participate actively in a mentoring relationship as it unfolds. I have chosen each piece of correspondence featured in the following pages specifically because it highlights a common theme in eating disorders recovery—an issue, challenge, or opportunity that my mentees have faced that bears the gift of stronger recovery once it is successfully faced and overcome.

Structurally, each chapter presents one single piece of correspondence—one letter from a mentee and my response to her letter—and then gives you the chance through a "Recovery Workshop" to learn and apply the very same tools and techniques I first employed successfully in my own recovery and have since shared with my mentees in turn. Finally, immediately following each workshop, you will find a "Life Celebration Affirmation," an affirming statement or set of statements designed specifically to train your mind to *want* recovery, to *believe in* recovery, and to *strive for* recovery as determinedly as you do.

Before beginning to read through each chapter, you may want to have a journal handy, or even to choose a special "Beating ANA" journal to use just to complete the Workshop exercises. In addition, I highly recommend actually speaking each affirmation aloud to yourself and then writing it out in your journal. In this way, you can tell yourself, tell yourself, and tell yourself again—aurally, visually, kinetically—that recovery is possible, and you *are* worth doing the hard work of recovery for!

You will quickly notice that my mentoring relationships are very hands-on—I believe in combining the power of understanding and application in order to derive full benefit from the hard work recovery requires. So now, prepare yourself to dig in, work harder than you've ever worked before, invest *everything* that you have into working through each chapter's material right along with me and my mentees, and then expect to reap the full rewards as you begin to meet your recovery goals!

It is also important for me to share with you that serving as a mentor has been a continual source of strength and renewal for me in my own recovery as well. Each letter I respond to presents a new challenge and opportunity for me to both share and also more firmly own what I have already achieved. Each mentee who allows me the privilege of offering my support gives me another chance to choose recovery and another opportunity to practice for myself what I am asking her to examine.

Notably, over the years I have noticed that my mentees often begin to express their desire to mentor others even while they are still in the midst of their own recovery work. This is a noble calling and yet also one that requires our full respect for the role a mentor plays in the life of someone who is struggling. It has been my experience that we can help others best when we help ourselves first—so keep in mind that for each day that you choose recovery, do the hard work your own recovery requires, and learn the lessons your mentor has to share, you are *already* helping others who want to heal as well!

Ultimately, when properly approached, with each aspect of a mentoring relationship experienced at its appropriate time, the mentoring relationship shows itself to be a beautiful cycle of giving and receiving, receiving and giving—on either side of the cycle, everybody wins!

Introducing the Contributors
(aka My Mentees)

Before we venture forward together into the chapters ahead, I want to take a moment to introduce you to five of the most courageous women I know: Nadia, Michelle, Jenna, Krista, and Lori. In age, they range from late teens to almost forty. In spirit they are timeless—locked tenaciously in varying stages of their shared heroic, life-or-death battle with the eating disorder within.

Although all of these women were willing to allow their correspondence to be published under their real names, I have assigned each a pseudonym, believing it best for them to remain anonymous for the sake of their continued progress in recovery. Some are still living as a dependent under another's wing, and others are mothers themselves, fighting to maintain the delicate balance between reparenting themselves and bringing up the next generation.

All five women have remained steadfastly committed to working out the details of their own recovery, no matter how long it takes. For that, for the gift of their correspondence here, and for their belief in me, you, and themselves, I am eternally grateful. Nadia, Michelle, Jenna, Krista, and Lori are every woman—every *person*—struggling to recover from an eating disorder, and they are also utterly unique.

And in each of their stories you will most assuredly find some essential missing pieces of your own.

Part Two

ED, A.A., AND ME

In the tradition of the world-renowned fellowship of
Alcoholics Anonymous, the backbone for achieving
recovery success for many people lies in working through
a Twelve-Step program of recovery with their sponsor.
However, when my friend and sponsor, Lynn, first
approached me with the possibility (I think she used the
word "necessity") of me working through the Twelve Steps,
I was confused. I did not know at the time that in addition
to addressing problems with drinking, the Twelve Steps
have been and continue to be successfully applied to
conditions as diverse as gambling, substance abuse,

codependency, binge-spending . . . and eating disorders.

Lynn explained to me that, collectively, the Steps offer one way to address deep and overarching issues of shame, accountability, forgiveness, and renewed connection—work that must be done in every successful recovery program. This work is often too scary and painful to be done alone, but becomes much more possible and successful when done with the guidance and compassion of a sponsor who has first worked all Twelve Steps through with her own sponsor.

Over time, my personal experience working the Steps has shown me that Lynn was right. For instance, when Lynn and I began to explore the shame and regret I felt for things that had happened in my past, she shared that she too had struggled similarly, which helped me to not feel so alone. Then, we worked together to resolve those issues through asking for and receiving forgiveness wherever appropriate—even and especially if the forgiveness I needed was from myself.

Once Lynn and I had completed that part of my Step work together, she was then able to assist me with building new coping techniques to replace the old. Ultimately, I emerged from our work together free to build a life of health, wholeness, and service to others that no longer included an addiction to alcohol, an eating disorder, unhealthy relationships, or any other coping pattern that could harm me or those around me.

While it is highly recommended that you work through each Step in order as Lynn and I have done, there are many other excellent books devoted exclusively to the A.A. Twelve-Step process. I highly recommend the book *Alcoholics Anonymous* (also known as "The Big Book") if you want to learn more, since the Twelve Steps will not be our focus in this book.

Rather, we will turn all of our attention and energy in this section to constructing a firm foundation for your recovery work. In the tradition of Alcoholics Anonymous, it is widely maintained that building a foundation for success in recovery begins with working the First Step, because this is where you will determine whether or not you are ready to do whatever it takes to get better, and you will identify for yourself why you are choosing recovery. I also suspect that this is the reason why Lynn was so insistent we not move forward into the other Steps (which my perfectionist, task-oriented ED mind just *hated*!) until I had thoroughly completed my First Step.

Therefore, in the letters and exercises presented in each one of the chapters that follow, we will explore, through my mentees' eyes, a different facet of what it means to take your "First Step," examining it from the perspective of your health, life, significant relationships, dreams and hopes, and goals and plans for your life and future. When you emerge from this process, you will have had an opportunity to choose recovery in every area of your life.

Exciting, isn't it! And just a little hint to get you started in the right direction—in taking your First Step, take good care to choose well. Choose life. Choose *you*. You are worth taking this first big Step toward recovery. And remember, if I could do it, then *so can you*!

The "First Step"

Hi Shannon—

I am very torn right now. I want to get better, but I don't want to give the anorexia up. I don't know how to live without the anorexia. I want to be "normal" and get this disease out of my mind, but it is so hard to let go. Right now I am one pound away from hospitalization. If I lose one more pound, I will be in the hospital. I would rather die than go into the hospital again. I've been trying hard to eat a healthy diet, but I feel so guilty and I end up purging a few minutes later. I feel like my body won't allow me to eat. I don't know what to do to help me get into recovery. I am going to the doctor weekly and seeing a therapist, but it's not helping. The hospital triggers me more because there are so many skinny girls there. In the hospital they take all control away from me and then when I get out of the hospital I want that control back because they took it away for so long. So when I get out of the hospital, I usually lose a lot of weight. I would like to try recovery, but I don't know what the first step is.

Lori

Hi Lori—

I understand. And this is not going to be easy—no, it won't be. But is the way you are living right now really any easier? Consider carefully how you will spend that last pound, and accept responsibility for the choice you make, either way. It might sound strange, but I suspect that if you can do this, it will actually make you feel *better*. You may get your first real taste of hope in a very, very long time, and take the first step (because this is the first step) toward choosing life again.

Shannon

RECOVERY WORKSHOP

In the Twelve Step tradition of Alcoholics Anonymous, the First Step is the foundation of recovery, and it states, "We admitted we were powerless over alcohol—that our lives had become unmanageable."

In the same way, despite our best intentions and efforts otherwise, in time, our dependence on our eating disorder—both physiologically and psychologically—renders us essentially powerless to engage in the rest of our lives, at least in any way that matters.

If we do not recognize this—if we do not step into the ring, fold our hands, and bow with great respect to our worthy and formidable adversary—we will not stand a chance to heal. The reason for this is simple. Once we acknowledge that a problem exists, we begin to practice honesty. Where honesty is present, humility arises. And in humility, we are finally open enough to ask for and accept help.

Your assignment for this Workshop is simple. And it is also very difficult. I am, of course, going to ask you to write out the First Step for yourself, substituting "eating disorder" for "alcohol." But it will be a useless exercise to undertake until you have intellectually and emotionally comprehended the truth of this statement for yourself.

So spend some time getting acquainted with the feeling of profound powerlessness that arises when the eating disorder takes over your thoughts, cravings, and actions.

Ponder the First Step thoroughly until you can begin to see evidence of it at work in your life. Take a road trip back to each one of the times and places where you vowed to end your dependence on your eating disorder once and for all, only to fall helplessly and inevitably back into its patiently waiting arms.

Then ask and answer for yourself this one essential question: "Can I stop my dependence on the disordered eating behavior patterns on my own?"

Only after you have arrived at your own answer to this question is it finally time to write out the following statement for yourself: *I admit that I am powerless over my eating disorder—that my life has become unmanageable.*

In your admission of powerlessness lies tremendous power. In admitting your own weakness, you gain your first real access to your own strength. Your body may be weaker than you would wish, but understand this: your mind is pure, solid iron will.

Forge that iron into pure steel, and run its sharp blade through your eating disorder once and for all.

Take your life back. It starts by taking your very First Step.

Life Celebration Affirmation:

We can only go so long dragging our heels about regaining our self-respect. Eventually, we would rather lie down and die than live another day without it—that is how exhausting it is to keep up our own brave face to the face we see reflected back to us in the mirror.

You need your energy for worthier battles. You have the fight of a lifetime on your hands—conserve, conserve, conserve. It has probably not escaped your attention that within the First Step statement lies the loaded cannon of the word *powerless*. Do not let your eating disorder take this word, and your hand, and run away to dangerous places. Remind yourself that, in the word *powerless*, also resides the word *power*.

When your mind is tempted to believe that powerless is all you ever have been, are now, or ever will be, instead affirm for yourself these or similar words:

I am only powerless when I refuse to acknowledge the power that my eating disorder has over me. Once I do this, I gain access to an inexhaustible source of strength and power. In completing my First Step, I receive the strength to ask for and accept help. I enter into the well-populated world of those striving with all their might for recovery and realize that I am not alone anymore! By walking willingly into a place where so many courageous warriors dwell, I become strong enough to acknowledge that I too have something that I struggle with, something that I cannot overcome by remaining alone in my eating disorder's presence. Now that I have accepted the role of student of the art and discipline of recovery, I access the potential to someday be a master in my own right!

The H.O.W. of Recovery (Honesty-Openness-Willingness)

Hi Shannon—

My anorexia started when I was ten years old, and it kept getting worse over the years. I was hospitalized at age twelve and was doing well for a while. I relapsed at age fourteen and lost a lot of weight and things kept getting worse from there. I've been hospitalized three times in the last two years. It feels like I am stuck in a cycle of relapsing and then going into the hospital. I can't seem to find the strength to recover. My body isn't in good condition and my bones and muscles are starting to disintegrate. And even though my body is falling apart, I cannot overcome my anorexia. It gets stronger every day, and all I can do is watch. I would appreciate any support or advice that you could give me.

Lori

Hi Lori—

I always tell those I work with that as long as you're still breathing, you're still doing okay—you still have hope. You're still hanging on. I don't know why you haven't given up, haven't given in yet; I don't know why you haven't just said to your eating disorder, "Okay, you win." But I believe that *you do know*, and that acknowledging it to yourself is the key to finally gaining the upper hand.

Shannon

RECOVERY WORKSHOP

An eating disorder places a curiously strong yet initially invisible barrier between you and your life. When in the grips of a powerful mental disease such as an eating disorder, it is easy to plead ignorance to and innocence of the factors leading us to our own demise. We convince ourselves that we are but spectators at our own funeral, powerless to do more than watch as events unfold to their logical conclusion. We continually allow ourselves to be made sport of—to be bullied and intimidated by reminders of the gratuitous violence we have inflicted upon ourselves. We stare at the shrapnel, the open wounds, the fading scars that our battle with our eating disorder has generated, until they are all we can see.

We do not yet see the truth. We do not yet perceive that, even as our inexplicable, indescribable self-torture escalates, and even when the eating disorder rolls out the big guns, we are *still here*.

If we want to win this war, to free the refugee—us—from the unmentionable prisoner-of-war life we have been enduring, we have got to find a way to psych ourselves back into the game!

In the Alcoholics Anonymous tradition, it is said that there are three key ingredients you must cultivate in order to do this. These three things are the "H.O.W" of recovery. They are, in this order:

1. Honesty: objectively looking at your life and seeing what is broken and who can fix it

2. Openness: being open to believing that the way life has been doesn't dictate the future

3. Willingness: the "I will do whatever it takes" attitude that sustained recovery requires

So, for your assignment for this Workshop, journal about these three elements, asking yourself whether or not you feel that you have each quality and have it in sufficient measure to commit to healing and to your own life.

It may seem that it should be enough to acknowledge that we are still here, still breathing, still living within the realm of hope for our eventual full recovery. But it really is not: not until we understand the mechanics of H.O.W. can we take action on that hope to achieve what we are hoping for—lasting recovery. We take action when we have the honesty to admit that things are still broken, despite our best efforts otherwise. We take action when we hold ourselves continually open to new techniques, remaining resolutely receptive to new sources of support and new feeds of information. We take action when we are willing, in each new moment, to try again.

H.O.W. are you going to overcome your eating disorder?

If at first you do not succeed, get up, get up, get up, and try again!

Life Celebration Affirmation:

The human body has amazing recuperative and regenerative powers. We have stories, preserved for us by historians, of the extreme deprivation endured in concentration camps by victims of the Holocaust, and we have corresponding tales of their survival and triumph in the face of incredible odds. These stories prove to us that our bodies are literally built to last, to restore, to adjust.

But it does us no good if we fail to remember this. The next time you are tempted to get discouraged about your body's ability to survive damage caused by your disease, stop your mind in its tracks and lead it instead to affirm these or similar words:

I am a living being, and I dwell in a powerful fortress called the body. My body is my bodyguard; it is charged with doing whatever it takes to preserve my life and keep me safe. If it has to take a beating for a while as I battle my eating disorder, it will do so, willingly and without complaint, if it can deflect the brunt of the disease from harming the occupant within: me. Thank you, body, for all you have suffered through on my behalf. I am honestly open to and willing to do whatever it takes to learn to take better care of us both. Thank you for your faithful service to me. I call you my true friend and call upon you for continued support as we beat back the assault of the eating disorder together, once and for all!

Eating Is Not Optional

Dear Shannon—

The cafeteria here at my college is open from 11:30 to one o'clock for lunch, which makes it impossible for me to get there to eat because of my class schedule. This presents a problem. And eating on my way to class . . . I have this issue that I really can't eat unless I'm sitting down. As for eating in class . . . I don't want to do it. I can't do it. Even if I were allowed, I *can't* do it. Another issue is the options for me in our cafeteria when I do get a chance to go. My choices are basically limited to salad or cheese breadsticks, which are actually not good, put nicely.

Michelle

Hi Michelle—

One thing I am picking up on in your latest e-mail is a sense that you are beginning to approach your continued recovery as if eating is optional. It may be difficult, it may be awkward, it may be embarrassing, it may put you in the public eye more than you would like, but *eating is not optional*.

Skipping a meal for someone without an eating disorder is just that—skipping a meal. It may be unpleasant but necessary. And it is quickly released when the option to eat arises. For someone with an eating disorder, however, skipping a meal is a lifestyle choice. It would be like saying that abstaining from alcohol is optional for an alcoholic—like saying that it is at their discretion. It is not. It is up to the individual to realize that the moment the abuse recommences, the vicious cycle begins again.

Shannon

RECOVERY WORKSHOP

It is simple, really. We have to eat to live. I must eat if I want to live. You too must consume food and hydrating liquids to keep your physical body alive, much like you fuel a car to keep it running.

And yet the very simplicity of this fact is what makes it so easy to disregard! We can come up with every excuse in the book for why we cannot fit the necessity of a meal into our day. Or why we need to squash them all into one long secret "meal" we call a binge. Or why what goes in at mealtimes must immediately come back out again—preferably before any of the nutrients have been absorbed.

In this Workshop, the first part of your assignment is to make a list of all the excuses you have ever used to avoid the simple fact that *eating is not optional.*

When your list is complete, get out a new page. Rewrite each excuse on your list, but this time add the words " . . . but eating is not optional" to the end of each sentence. From now on, each time your mind begins to hand you a plausible sounding reason for ignoring or abusing food, add " . . . but eating is not optional" to the end of it, and revise your plans accordingly.

In the second part of your assignment, visualize yourself in the following scenario:

You are driving down the street when you look down at your gas gauge and —oh, no!—realize the red light is on. The arrow is sitting squarely on "empty." You look around, panicked. You spy a gas station on the next corner, and relief floods through you. "Whew," you think to yourself, "that was a close call." You pull up to the gas pump, insert your credit card, and lift the handle to begin fueling. You peer down inside the empty gas tank. "Oh, why bother?" you say to yourself. You close the gas door, get back in your car, and drive away, red warning light still flashing brightly.

Would you ever do this in real life? Does it boggle your mind— the thought of driving on an empty tank, refusing to refuel, and still expecting your car to take you wherever you want to go? (Similarly, how likely would it be that, were you to fill your tank to "full" and then keep on filling it, that the excess fuel would find a way to fit inside usefully, rather than spilling over the sides to create a potentially hazardous condition for you?)

So, then, why do we so often over- or underfill our "tank" when it comes to the "fuel" we put into our body, when, in the very same way that gas is fuel for our car . . . FOOD IS FUEL FOR OUR BODY.

The next time you head to the kitchen, determined to eat

responsibly rather than too much or not at all, visualize your stomach as if it is your car's gas tank. Imagine filling it to just the right amount—choosing the perfect combination of nutrients to get you to where you want to go.

Refuel no more and no less than this amount. Then, leave the kitchen and "drive" away.

Life Celebration Affirmation:

I still vividly remember the day I walked into the Volkswagen dealership, chomping at the bit to trade in my faithful, dependable, eleven-year-old Toyota for a flashy new Turbo VW Beetle. In my cautious, scientific fashion, I evaluated the choices before me ... "Hey, Dad, look! That blue Beetle matches my toenail polish perfectly!"

Three years later, I was trading in the second of two new Beetles as a certified "lemon" for—you guessed it—a faithful, dependable Toyota. I have never once looked back.

Eating responsibly for your body's needs is a simple, surefire way to get from here to there, from A to B (and, in time, to Z as well). It is not flashy, dramatic, or exciting. It is in no way extreme—unlike bingeing and purging or starving.

But it is what works.

When you doubt that you can ever relearn how to accomplish this utterly mundane but oh-so-necessary task, repeat these or similar words:

I am at the gas pump, and my gas gauge is on "empty." I am now refueling my tank—no more nor less than what it requires to take me where I want and need to go. Now, I refuel. When I am done, I drive away to once more engage in my life, reenergized and refreshed. I do not have to worry about the next time I will be required to refuel. I will know when the time is right and how much fuel my body requires for the next leg of our journey. My body is trustworthy and reliable. It knows what type of energy it needs to run properly, and it knows how much of this energy it needs. Together, we can do this. Together, we are an unstoppable team!

Getting Smart About Eating Disorders

Hi Shannon—

Although the scale tells me I'm underweight, I look in the mirror and what I see makes me sick to my stomach. At first I didn't totally understand it, but the feeling that I had the choice to eat or not eat, to throw up or not throw up, felt like it was *my choice*. I was in control but out of control (if that makes sense). I struggle with food every day. I fight the voices but as soon as ED gets a foothold it takes over like it has now. By falling into what the ED tells me, I feel like I have accomplished some great goal; although in my logical thought I know how unhealthy it is and the risks I'm taking by doing this, the fear of gaining more weight overrides any sense of logical thought.

Jenna

Hi Jenna—

So, the first step you must take in your efforts to heal is to begin to disassociate *you now* from *you then*—to separate out your essential being or self from the body/mind of Jenna that developed the eating disorder to cope. Next, sit quietly for a few minutes and spontaneously brainstorm all of the things your eating disorder says to you that you can think of—just remember all the times when you've stood in front of a mirror or felt a hunger pang or went to reach for something to eat, only to hear the ED voice kick in to stop you. Then write down whatever it said. Start to learn how the voice attacks you, and then learn your own countermoves.

Shannon

RECOVERY WORKSHOP

Have you ever heard the old saying that has become so popular in *Alcoholics Anonymous* circles: "The definition of insanity is doing the same thing over and over again expecting different results"?

I will confess that I had heard it many times before it sank in that it also referred to me! At that point, I realized that if I wanted to get different results, then I too was going to have to *try different things*.

Eating disorders are brain disorders. While there are a host of interesting theories as to why the brains of eating disorder victims may function differently from other brains in the presence of certain stressors, the fact remains that eating disorders are mental illnesses. Period. The end. They cannot be reasoned with. They do not make sense to outside observers or even to the victims themselves when on the outside looking in. Yet, we know now that whether they make logical sense or not, they are dangerously real.

When my brother was born with a congenital leg deformity which caused his left leg to be four inches shorter than his right, his doctors, parents, sister, and friends did not yell at him for his inability to "will" his leg to grow faster. He did not yell at himself for failing to do so. Instead, his treatment team and family went to work with him to fix the problem.

We have already learned that any attempt to rationalize or reason with the inner voice of the ED is fruitless. Eating disorders are considered by many to be anosognosic ("sleep-inducing") diseases. They cause their victim to cultivate the ability to rationalize or even ignore behaviors around food that a person with healthy brain function would never permit themselves to engage in. In addition, exposure to the often severe malnutrition or nutritional imbalances that an eating disorder demands changes brain chemistry to the point where black appears white and wrong appears right.

Part of eating disorder recovery involves what is commonly called "refeeding" or "weight stabilization" (see the next chapter for more on this process). This first phase of refeeding the body, while very challenging for victims and their loved ones, restores adequate nutrient levels to stabilize brain function, which allows for recovery work to begin on other levels. The second phase involves what I call "getting smart"—refeeding the brain with accurate information about the origins, causes, and possible solutions for overcoming the disease so that when the ED voice speaks we are less likely to listen and react.

For this Workshop, your assignment comes in two parts. In this first part, you will begin to "get smart" about the biological foundations of your disease, so that you can equip your powerful mind with ammunition to overwhelm the inaccurate inner ED voice with the facts. Read and carefully consider the following three articles and then journal your thoughts:

1. "Starvation and Behavior" (http://www.joyproject.org/overcoming/starvation.html)

2. "An evolutionary explanation for anorexia?" (http://www.apa.org/monitor/apr04/anorexia.html)

3. "Fighting Anorexia: No One to Blame" (http://www.newsweek.com/id/51592)

Hopefully you are now beginning to perceive that the eating disorder is a master of disguise. But you can beat it at its own game. The healthy brain is a master sleuth. It thrives on accurate knowledge the way the body thrives on the nutrients found in food.

For instance, did you know that health professionals working in the field have identified a personality profile (see page 48) associated with a person who is at higher risk for developing an eating disorder? For this second part of your assignment, you will expand your knowledge base to include an understanding of the attributes that you—yes, you with the eating disorder—really possess.

Before you begin, however, allow me to introduce to you an amazing woman, Peggy Claude-Pierre, who has served as one of the pioneers in researching and identifying the true gifts that an eating disorder survivor has to share with the world. Peggy has her own triumphant story of recovery that is nothing short of miraculous. With no help or support from her local medical community, she devised a way to salvage the lives of both her daughters, each of whom had been diagnosed with a terminal eating disorder. In her bestselling book, *The Secret Language of Eating Disorders*, Peggy wrote about her experiences and how all that she learned about eating disorder recovery through her success with saving her daughters led to her decision to open her own treatment facility. In her book, she writes: "These [the lives of those who suffer from eating disorders] are lives to be cherished." Later on, she addresses readers who suffer from eating disorders directly, stating, "You are not failures at life, merely at understanding your own value."

Write out both of Peggy's statements in your journal. Then journal your own thoughts about each. How do you feel about these statements when you apply them to *yourself*? Do you believe yours is "a life to be cherished"? Do you see how it is possible that you could have failed, not at living your life, but at "understanding your own value"? Why or why not? How could you convince yourself that it might be true?

You can start to convince yourself through the exercise that follows, as you study each characteristic of your personality profile and begin to meet a you who is so worth saving. This exercise will take five journal pages. At the top of each page, write out one of the attributes listed below. Underneath each attribute, divide the page into two columns. In the column on the left, brainstorm ideas about how possessing that attribute might have led to the *development* of your eating disorder. In the column on the right, brainstorm ways you can use that attribute to help you *overcome* your eating disorder.

Keep in mind as you work through this exercise that I am not asking you to support or refute why each of the following five attributes does or does not describe you—or even to agree or disagree that you possess them. Rather, I am asking you to try them on for size—to explore how, if you did possess these qualities, they may at one time in your life have facilitated an atmosphere ripe for the development of an eating disorder, and how, if you did possess these same qualities now, they might facilitate an equally hospitable environment for recovery to take place. Adopting a detached sense of adventure and curiosity will allow you to sidestep any attempts on the part of the ED mind to make up your mind for you before you have had a chance to think through the attributes for yourself.

So now, without further delay, here are your five attributes (drum roll please . . .)

1. Above average to very high intelligence

2. Compassion and desire to contribute

3. Sensitive and caring

4. Commitment to excellence

5. Poor emotional coping skills and weak sense of self

"Getting smart" about your recovery means replacing the eating disorder's "facts" with real facts—like the fact that, given the scientifically sound list above, you are really a pretty terrific person with a lot of promise, potential, and possibility just waiting in the wings for you to acknowledge it! Only *one* of the five attributes (Hint: number five) even gives an inkling of a door left slightly ajar . . . just enough so an eating disorder might have crept through unnoticed.

But now, you notice. Your eyes are opened . . . your *mind* is opened. You have high intelligence. You want to do good. You care about others (and are learning to care about yourself). You have tons of energy, drive, and passion that are even now collectively wriggling free from beneath the weight of the eating disorder's demands. And right where your eating disorder attacked you is also the place where you have full power to get strong, by building up your healthy emotional coping skills and strengthening your sense of self-identity and self-worth.

So now you know how and where the thief of your life crept in. And you also know how to find and evict it—once and for always—by "getting smart" about the how, when, where, why, and who of your recovery. Happy hunting!

Life Celebration Affirmation:

The author Marianne Williamson writes in her book *A Return to Love*, "We ask ourselves, Who am I to be brilliant, gorgeous, talented, fabulous? Actually, who are you not to be?"

Who are you not to be? If you can think of even one other human being in your life whom you admire, look up to, and hope to emulate someday, that is how you know that you too have that very same ability to shine!

You can prove it to yourself by believing that you have what it takes to outsmart your eating disorder and choosing to take action on that belief. Paula Abdul, a spokeswoman for the National Eating Disorders Association (NEDA), received the highest honor NEDA bestows on an individual, the Profiles in Living Award. At a press conference held just prior to the formal presentation of her award, Paula told attendees, "I have received awards, but nothing like this. This is the true achievement in my life because I wouldn't have a life if I didn't get through this [bulimia]."

So when you, too, do this, when you beat your eating disorder once and for all, it will be the achievement of your lifetime. You will no longer doubt that you can do anything you put your powerful mind to. You will no longer doubt the truth of who you are.

But in the meantime, in those moments when you find that you are still in doubt—*temporary* doubt—affirm often these or similar words:

I am brilliant, gorgeous, handsome, beautiful, talented, and fabulous. I am overflowing with light. I do not fear my light—I embrace it. I follow it. It guides me through and out of the darkness from which the eating disorder voice calls to me. I am no longer afraid of that darkness because I have already experienced everything it has to offer me and I have decided that I am through dwelling there. My destiny and my legacy are of the light, and that is where I am going. I am even now on my way . . . my powerful, brilliant, gorgeous, handsome, beautiful, talented, and fabulous way!

The F.E.A.R. Factor (False Evidence Appearing Real)

Hi Shannon—

I'm really struggling. I mean, *really* struggling. I don't know what to do. It's like this— life would be a heck of a lot easier if we didn't have to eat, you know? I mean, I was talking about it with my mom yesterday, and we both agreed that it'd be easier to just take a pill or two, get all the nutrients you ever needed for the week, and not waste time and energy with the whole cooking, chewing, swallowing process. My health can't afford to be jeopardized by [not eating] again. . . . I am scared out of my mind. I feel so vulnerable. . . . I have no idea what I'm going to do. . . .

Michelle

Dear Michelle—

Yes, it would be easier if we didn't have to eat. But now you are aware of the difficulty of eating, and this means that the eating disorder is not stronger than you are anymore. With awareness comes responsibility and the requirement to exert superhuman strength to overcome. Now it gets harder. Now you ramp it up and meet that challenge head on. So you are right where you need to be, learning the exact lessons you need to learn. Don't shrink back. Stand up and fight!

Shannon

RECOVERY WORKSHOP

The definition of food for the larger population: *any substance that can be metabolized by an organism to give energy and build tissue.*

The definition of food for the eating-disordered population: *the very personification of fear.*

Every cell in our body craves it. Every neuron in our mind revolts against it. And we are caught in between—the proverbial rubber band, stretched to the breaking point.

In the Alcoholics Anonymous tradition, such mortal dilemmas are often categorized as "F.E.A.R.: False Evidence Appearing Real."

FACT: Food is a *must* for our body to survive.

F.E.A.R.: Food is a toxic substance that we must avoid at all costs.

The presence of F.E.A.R. is also why refeeding*—the process of nutritional stabilization by which you will begin to consume at least the minimum daily recommended allowance of calories and

---

* The ideal approach to refeeding is always to consult a dietician or nutritionist for help with constructing a daily plan that allows for intake of adequate amounts of each required nutrient.

nutrients to stabilize body, mind, and emotions before undertaking the hard work of recovery—is often the most tangibly, immediately difficult, painful, terrifying aspect of recovering from an eating disorder. I have seen grown women break down and cry when confronted with a plateful of innocent spaghetti. I myself have been known, back in my anorexic days, to panic at the perceived consequences of consuming both apples and pizza in the same sitting.

This phenomenon is why, when I first began attempts at teaching myself how to eat again, out of sheer desperation to follow through, I actually began carrying books about the nutritional value of food around with me to read during mealtimes. I "fed" my mind good thoughts about food, while I was using my newfound book knowledge** to make healthy food choices for my body as well. In this way, I began to align my mind's thoughts with my body's needs by giving myself mental ammunition to override the eating disorder's "facts" about my food choices and options with *real* factual information!

Now, I will be honest—this was an extremely difficult process for me to put myself through. It required me to actually pay attention to my "trigger" foods—foods that, when I was confronted with them, provoked such a negative, fear-based emotional response that I found myself unable to consume them. I had devised very strict rituals and routines to avoid contact with my trigger foods—rules about what I could eat and when, where, and

---

** It is important to involve a dietician or nutritionist in selecting nutrition-related information and reading materials that are appropriate to address your particular nutritional challenges and needs.

with whom I could eat it. And my eating disorder had made it very clear what its rules were about what I could not—could never, ever, ever, eat—without fear of dreadful reprisal. So attempting to become willing to even *consider* consuming food, let alone foods I was deathly afraid of, took tremendous courage!

Yet the fact remained that many of the foods that triggered me—foods like avocados and olive oil and cheese and yogurt— were the very same foods that were required to heal my body and my mind for the hard work of recovery. Other trigger foods, like candy and chips, were less difficult or necessary for me to immediately address since my body had no significant biological need for the nutrients they contained. It is also important to acknowledge that your trigger foods and my trigger foods may not be the same, and that you may not feel triggered by the same foods all the time. For instance, some foods may prove triggering only when you find yourself under emotional stress but provoke no response in you when you are feeling calm.

The critical issue when addressing trigger foods is to identify those that your body needs (which will always be ones that fall into the United States Department of Agriculture's Food Pyramid's six major categories: grains, vegetables, fruits, oils, milk, meats/beans) that are also foods you, for one reason or another, feel unwilling to consume at all or in sufficient quantity to meet your body's nutrient needs.

So it is within this framework that we will embark upon this chapter's two-part exercise:

Part One: Confronting the F.E.A.R. Journal for yourself how the *necessity* of consuming food in appropriate quantities with balanced (six-food-group) nutrients is masked by the presence of F.E.A.R. in your life. This is an exercise you may want to take several days to complete. Pay special attention at snack and mealtimes to the messages you hear in your head as you go to the kitchen, head to the table, or choose and prepare your own snacks and meals. Pay especially close attention to foods that your eating disorder says "no" to. (For instance, every time I reached for an avocado—and I *love* avocados—my eating disorder voice would say, "If you eat that, it is going to make you as big as the Goodyear Blimp.") So now, turn to a blank page in your journal, and label it "F.E.A.R. Messages." Then, each time you hear a message from your ED mind that relates to a particular food item that you know belongs to one of the six food groups and is thus healthy, or is a food item you have been specifically told your body requires, write it down. Any time you hear a message related to consuming food in general (for example, if it is breakfast time and your eating disorder says to you, "If you eat that piece of toast, you will have to restrict for the rest of the day to make up for it . . ."), write it down in your journal.

Part Two: Consuming the FACTs. Once you have at least five consistent F.E.A.R.-based messages identified, it is time to put them to the test. Take a look at each message in its turn. Does it make logical sense? Is the implied threat or consequence even biologically *possible*? Let's take the message about my avocado as an example. In no world I know of would the consumption of one avocado provoke a human body to instantly expand to become the size of the Goodyear Blimp. But for many years I took F.E.A.R. as fact and avoided avocados like the plague. Similarly, I don't know of a human body alive on this earth presently whose caloric daily requirement consists of one slice of toast. But it was not uncommon for me to take this F.E.A.R. as fact each morning while making my breakfast food choices! So for each F.E.A.R. message you have identified, write out its corresponding FACT. In my avocado message, for instance, I learned to counteract my F.E.A.R. by reminding myself of the following FACT: "Avocados are a source of good fat to strengthen my ligaments and tendons so I can play music again." In this way, I was able to begin consuming avocados and then many other valuable, nutritious foods as well. This allowed my body to heal, my mind to strengthen, and, over time, paved the way for me to resume my music career and my life again—free from my eating disorder's influence!

Please understand—I do realize that in this exercise we are confronting the fundamental coping behavior that characterizes an eating disorder—the use or misuse of food for purposes other than to maintain your body's physical health and well-being. It is tempting (or at least it was for me when I stood in your shoes) to decide to skip this lesson or maybe work around it for a while, until you feel "ready." But I will challenge you not to make that choice— because the fact is that as long as your eating disorder is in control of your food intake, you will never feel "ready" to eat—or to do the exercises in this chapter!

If you want to recover from your eating disorder, F.E.A.R. notwithstanding, there is no way to get around it—you simply must learn how to properly, responsibly consume a balanced diet. If I could do it, if I could learn how to tune out the F.E.A.R.-based messages my eating disorder sent me about food and start eating responsibly and healthfully again through learning and practicing the FACTs, then I am confident that you *can too.*

Life Celebration Affirmation:

Think of how Christopher Columbus must have felt in those first few moments when he spotted land, thinking he had at last found his western route to Asia, not realizing that his discovery was not simply a new route, but rather a whole new world.

You probably will try many things before you find the exact formula that works for you. And it may be years before you realize the true significance of your discoveries. But in the meantime, you will be healing. You will be joining the ranks of the greatest adventurers, willing to endure immeasurable risk for the promise of linking arms with the immortal minority who have earned the right to count overcoming an eating disorder as amongst their greatest life accomplishments.

You will not be able to endure the F.E.A.R. that arises when you determine to undergo this arduous journey, let alone stay your courageous course through to the end, without both single-minded purpose and the help of practical tools to overcome obstacles in your path. When your courage and energy are flagging, when you doubt your own sanity in even attempting such a feat, affirm continuously these or similar words:

If I could endure the living death of an eating disorder, I can endure any amount of F.E.A.R. and hardship on my road to overcoming it. I am a pioneer, journeying to places within myself that have long since been sealed off and declared disaster zones, and in the process I am discovering new lands I didn't even know existed! I am not a disaster zone or a stranger in a strange land—and no part of me is off-limits to myself. I will go where no one—not even me—has been before. I will eat responsibly again someday—one day—soon—today. The FACT is that I will survive this. I will recover. I can recover. I am recovering—even now, I can see land at last. Even now, I approach my brave new world!

Flavor of the Month

Dear Shannon—

I will tell you honestly that I know that I now drink too often. Just wine, but generally every night and several water-glass-sized drinks. I'm starting to look forward to it way too much, which is probably not a good thing, but I at least wait until evening.

Nadia

Dear Nadia—

You land on something else that I've also struggled with in recovery— the transference from one addictive pattern to another. You are in essence avoiding making further progress toward your recovery from your eating disorder with your newfound interest in alcohol—I've done the same in that I used bulimia, and later alcohol, and still later relationships, as a way to limit or manage my need for restricting. But ultimately, I had to give it all up in order to get my life back again.

Shannon

RECOVERY WORKSHOP

Addiction transference, as I mention in my letter to Nadia, is a phenomenon where one or more subsidiary addictive coping patterns emerge simultaneously with the primary concern, or, even worse, just as progress is being made in the area of primary concern—in this case, Nadia's eating disorder! This constant "transference" from one addictive pattern to the other, and back again, prevents the person from making a full and complete recovery from the need for *any* form of addictive coping behavior to manage the stresses of daily life.

Let me elaborate. When I was little, my dad used to take me to Baskin-Robbins after his weekly voice lesson. I'm not sure exactly who the reward was for (being as how we seemed to suffer equally through his lessons), but we sure looked forward to it! These trips were always "our little secret" . . . nothing Mom really needed to know about.

Aside from my unwavering loyalty to mint chocolate chip, I was nevertheless pulled into indecision at least one trip out of every four by the "flavor of the month"—the newest, hottest thing. Even if it was some gut-wrenching combination like rum-punch raisin or raspberry-mint bubble gum, the temptation remained. Something new. Something I hadn't tried before. Something I might like.

Addiction transference is a similar phenomenon. Articles, papers, and whole books have been written about this destructive shift in loyalty from one addictive behavioral pattern to another. For instance, in 2004, in a seventy-three-page report entitled "Food for Thought: Substance Abuse and Eating Disorders," the National Center on Addiction and Substance Abuse revealed that up to 35 percent of alcohol or drug abusers also have an eating disorder, compared to 3 percent of the general population.

When we are little, maybe what we are attempting to give up is mint chocolate chip. When we are older, maybe it is anorexia. Or bulimia. Or binge eating. Or all of the above. Maybe it then becomes alcohol, or other people, or prescription drugs.

But ultimately, what we are really attempting to do is a feat of the highest order—to give up the *need for the addictive behaviors themselves.*

This takes time. Patience. Self-effort. Some measure of grace toward ourselves, and also from others who have stood in our shoes and can remind us that we are not alone in how we feel or in the enormity of our task.

Your first assignment for this Workshop is to identify the different ways you become triggered emotionally, and the various ways you try to overcome your dependency on your eating disorder by transferring the addictive behavioral patterns from one habit-forming disorder to another—with the end result being that you are never able to totally give up your need for the addictive behaviors themselves. So now:

1. Create for yourself a "Top Ten" list of triggers, by which I mean daily or occasional life stressors that cause you to seek out eating-disordered or other addictive behaviors to cope.

2. Create a "Top Ten" list of all of the addictive coping behaviors you have turned to when you are triggered.

With these lists, you are priming your mind to become aware of potentially triggering situations, interactions, or experiences before you become fully enveloped in them, and then to become equally aware of the knee-jerk reaction ways you usually try to cope with being triggered. You can think of these lists like your "Early Warning System"—the storm is still approaching, but now you can start to see the clouds gathering before they open up over your head. In this way, you will give yourself time to choose a new way to address your triggers—one that doesn't involve doing anything on your "addictive coping behaviors" list!

Your second assignment is to identify alternatives to the addictive behaviors by creating a list of new, healthy coping skills that you can use when you get triggered. There is no limit to the number of items you can add to your list, and the only restriction is that each item must foster a sense of confidence, safety, and peace within you, without using a substance, drink, eating-disordered coping skill, another person in a way that is detrimental to either of you, or any resources you may have on hand that would do you or others harm.

Sound like a tall order? I have confidence that you can do it—and to prove it, I will share my ever-expanding list of coping methods with you. I like to call my list "Calming Things," and on it you will find the following: music (writing, playing, singing, or listening), meditation, a hot bath or shower, taking long walks, yoga, reading a good book, taking deep breaths, calling a friend to talk *and* listen, jogging at the park, experiencing nature, watching a good movie or my favorite TV shows, playing with my beautiful pet bird, Pearl, cleaning my house, volunteering, writing poetry or doing anything creative, visiting an art gallery or museum, spending time with my friends and family, hot tea or coffee (my favorite thing!), taking a nap, affirmations, going to therapy, burning a candle or incense, watching my two pet fish, Gill and Bob, and paying kind attention to myself. Every week I add more to the list, and I have been doing this for several years now! I use my list if I ever find that I feel triggered and my brain freezes and I forget what to do to calm myself. I actually keep my list stored in my phone so wherever I am, it is always with me.

So begin your list now, and add to it every chance you get. Then use it whenever you need it to stabilize yourself during moments of stress, so that you can give yourself the chance to make *consistent* progress toward all of your recovery goals.

Maybe when you were little you thought you liked mint chocolate chip. Or anorexia. Or laxatives. Or ten packages of chocolate chip cookies in one sitting.

But today, maybe your preferences have changed. Your "flavor of the month"—of *every* month—may now be recovery.

Life Celebration Affirmation:

I still like mint chocolate chip (in fact, I may even have a scoop when I am done writing this chapter!). But it does not rule my life. I do not run to it when I am stressed or to the white ceramic god when my eating-disordered brain suggests I might have had too much of it. It is just what it is—an innocent scoop of ice cream—today's still-delicious remnants of a pre-anorexic little girl's good memories.

Today, I run to affirmations of self-worth when I am stressed. When I crave a set of addictive behaviors, I turn to repeating my affirmations. I have found that this is the healthiest of all "addictions"—affirming positive statements for myself, my present and future, my own self-confidence and esteem, and the valued relationships in my life.

The next time you are feeling overwhelmed by the demands of life, other people, the dinner table, or anything else, pause and take time to repeat these or similar words:

I am addicted to life. I am addicted to treating myself well, and to improving my health, my life, and all the people in it—starting with me. My "flavor of the month" is practicing all the different ways I can love myself. Every month, every day—today—the flavor of love is just as delicious, just as satisfying, and just as fulfilling. Over time, with each small step forward that I take, this flavor will permeate every dish I prepare and eat, and it will nourish all of me in all of the ways that the addictive behaviors could never even pretend to do. Today and every day, I can more easily spot the ways that the ED tries to morph and trick me into letting it back into my life. Today and every day, I slowly, steadily, replace my need for it with healthier, happier coping skills. I am beginning to see now that I am smarter than my ED—by far. And I will not—I do not—let it back in!

READER/CUSTOMER CARE SURVEY

HEFG

We care about your opinions! Please take a moment to fill out our online Reader Survey at **http://survey.hcibooks.com**.
As a **"THANK YOU"** you will receive a **VALUABLE INSTANT COUPON** towards future book purchases
as well as a **SPECIAL GIFT** available only online! Or, you may mail this card back to us.

First Name _____ MI. _____ Last Name _____

Address _____ City _____

State _____ Zip _____ Email _____

1. Gender
- ☐ Female   ☐ Male

2. Age
- ☐ 8 or younger
- ☐ 9-12   ☐ 13-16
- ☐ 17-20   ☐ 21-30
- ☐ 31+

3. Did you receive this book as a gift?
- ☐ Yes   ☐ No

4. Annual Household Income
- ☐ under $25,000
- ☐ $25,000 - $34,999
- ☐ $35,000 - $49,999
- ☐ $50,000 - $74,999
- ☐ over $75,000

5. What are the ages of the children living in your house?
- ☐ 0 - 14   ☐ 15+

6. Marital Status
- ☐ Single
- ☐ Married
- ☐ Divorced
- ☐ Widowed

7. How did you find out about the book?
(please choose one)
- ☐ Recommendation
- ☐ Store Display
- ☐ Online
- ☐ Catalog/Mailing
- ☐ Interview/Review

8. Where do you usually buy books?
(please choose one)
- ☐ Bookstore
- ☐ Online
- ☐ Book Club/Mail Order
- ☐ Price Club (Sam's Club, Costco's, etc.)
- ☐ Retail Store (Target, Wal-Mart, etc.)

9. What subject do you enjoy reading about the most?
(please choose one)
- ☐ Parenting/Family
- ☐ Relationships
- ☐ Recovery/Addictions
- ☐ Health/Nutrition
- ☐ Christianity
- ☐ Spirituality/Inspiration
- ☐ Business Self-help
- ☐ Women's Issues
- ☐ Sports

10. What attracts you most to a book?
(please choose one)
- ☐ Title
- ☐ Cover Design
- ☐ Author
- ☐ Content

FOLD HERE

Comments

The Key to Life

Hi Shannon—

I have dreams—things that I want to do with my life that I know aren't possible while I'm struggling with the eating disorder. I'm currently in a musical. Performing is the only thing I feel like I'm halfway good at, and it has always been my out. I use it as an escape, but now my escape isn't working. My vocals aren't nearly as strong or as clear as they have been, and my range is smaller [due to inadequate nutrition]. Music is my passion, and now I even fail in that area.

I don't know what to do—I fight my need for my eating disorder, but it seems the harder I try, the harder I fall!

Krista

Hi Krista—

I see so much of myself in you. Music was the one thing that kept me from just letting the eating disorder take over. I realized when the eating disorder took my ability to play, sing, and write music from me that if I didn't believe I was valuable inherently, at least I had something of value that kept my head above water—and I wanted it back. As long as I could write songs and play and sing, I at least had one small piece of my identity that wasn't totally wrapped up in the eating disorder.

Shannon

RECOVERY WORKSHOP

W e all have something worth living for—worth fighting for. I call that something a "key to life." When it goes missing, we notice. We resent the loss. We want it back.

The pivotal point comes when we realize that we cannot have both—our eating disorder and the rest of our life too. This is why you must locate your key to life. When you find it, that is the moment when you will know that you have what it takes to survive.

So your assignment for this Workshop is twofold. First, you will work on finding your key to life. Any of these methods may be helpful—do not hesitate to try any or all of them:

1. Remember when you were a child. What did you dream of doing with your life?

2. Analyze your aptitudes, skills, and passions—what are you naturally good at? Where have you focused your time and energy? What matters to you? Why do you get up in the morning? What keeps you going on even the hardest of days?

3. Ask members of your support team, friends, and family for their observations about what your strengths, aptitudes, and passions are.

4. Divide a journal page into six sections: Relational, Financial, Spiritual, Physical, Personal, and Professional. Under each heading, write down your overall goal for each area of your life.

5. Simply close your eyes, imagine you living life *free* from your eating disorder, and visualize yourself out there "doing your thing." Open your eyes and write down whatever comes to mind *first* as that "thing."

6. Reconsider the information presented in the chapter titled "The First Step" (see page 29). *Why* has your life become unmanageable? Is it just the overwhelming time commitment the eating disorder demands? What else could you, would you, be able to do or accomplish if your time was freed up from managing your eating disorder? Write down the "what else."

7. Imagine you are eighty years old. There is one thing you never got the chance to try or do during your lifetime, and now you regret the missed opportunity. What is that one thing?

Next, you will write out your "Statement of Intent to Recover"— your intention to choose your key to life over your eating disorder. Be sure to include your key to life in your Statement of Intent. Here is a template that you can adapt if it is helpful:

I am going to recover from my eating disorder, no matter how long it takes, how hard I have to work, how much money I have to spend, or how much I have to rearrange my other priorities in order to make recovery my number one priority. I will win my life back, so that I can _____ *(fill in your "key to life" here).*

Your key to life is your ticket to and your promise of freedom. Your "Statement of Intent to Recover" is your reminder that you hold that key.

So now, grab your key, and then begin to turn it.

Life Celebration Affirmation:

Although most people do not believe me, I am an introvert at heart. Yes, it is true—I am shy, really quite reserved actually, when I am not in the public eye.

What bolsters me and gives me courage when I meet new people is this one simple thought: *Right now, I am meeting the* only one *of this person who ever was, is now, or ever will be!*

You must remind yourself that you too are unrepeatable. Singular. Unique. When you are gone, this world will be missing the only one of someone who has ever existed. You must not deprive yourself of the chance to shine, to contribute, to use your voice, to *be*. You exist so that you can *live*. So, when your courage flags, when even the reminder of your "key to life" is not enough to haul you to your feet again, affirm these or similar words:

I am the only me who ever has been, is now, or ever will be. I am singular, unique, unrepeatable, irreplaceable. I am a mystery, a miracle, but even more importantly—I am me. I will save myself. I will preserve this historical phenomenon so that it does not die but will live on even after I depart to inspire others to take heart, live with courage, fight what opposes them, and triumph—just as I am triumphing now.

Part Three
ED AT THE MOVIES

I first became ill at the age of eleven. In the ensuing years, I found sanctuary, refuge, and, finally, rebirth in some of the greatest films of our time.

An eating disorder is a voracious disease. And nothing tastes more delicious to a developing eating disorder than its host's sense of self. Who am I? What do I stand for? What do I long for? Why am I here? *Surely* it is not to become consumed by an eating disorder?!

After a while, we no longer have the energy to remember the right answers to these crucial questions. This is when we have to find new ways to infuse ourselves with a *remembrance* of who we really are without our eating disorder, and a renewed hope and determination that *yes we can* wrest our lives back from the eating disorder's clutches once and for all!

One way we can do this is by feeding our minds and hearts with the empowering stories of others. As we've already discussed, mentoring is one way in which we are able to share stories and give and gain strength. But what I didn't know, in the years when I was so ill and struggling for recovery, was that when I watched and rewatched each of the movies that I loved, I was actually taking strength as well from the characters' courageous stories of triumph over personal adversity, and then using that strength to keep fighting my own battle for survival right alongside them. A motion picture mentoring process, if you will!

Once my feet were on more stable ground again, I realized that even celluloid mentors have the full power to convey courage and the promise of a better life, if we are willing to allow them to give us this gift.

Through the movies explored in the following chapters of this section, frame by frame I rediscovered and reclaimed the little pieces of personal identity that my eating disorder had selfishly appropriated for its own. Some films taught me how to fight. Some, in contrast, taught me when to lay low. Some of the characters literally borrowed my heart—so strong was my connection with their suffering and redemption.

But, unlike the eating disorder, they always gave it back again—stronger and better than before.

May they do the same for you.

8 Mile

Hey Shannon—

Okay, so I've officially been in college for four days and I am loving it. Well, I'm loving the college part. The eating … well, that is not going so well. I'm trying to have a positive attitude about it all, trying to do the right thing, and it's just not happening. It's like there's no one to hold me accountable, so I am finding myself feeling incapable of doing what I need to do. I mean, I know I'm capable, but I'm just not doing it. I'm feeling like a failure again, and I was so positive I was going to be okay. I guess I was wrong. I really don't want to become one of the statistics for relapsing in college. But I also don't want to have anyone here to hold me accountable because that would involve telling people about it and I really don't want my reputation to be "Michelle, that girl who's obsessed with her eating disorder."

I believe I am up a creek without a paddle. To put it bluntly, this sucks.

Michelle

Hi Michelle—

Everybody at your new school, just like at your old school, struggles with something. And the collective silence holds you all back. Yes, there is a community at your school, as at many other schools, which does not want to advance, heal, take the time, do the work. Those are the people who will not understand, who will criticize, who will attempt to throw more of the spotlight on you so there will be less of a spotlight on them. But there is another community who is working hard to recover, heal, and connect with others who, like them, are leaders. These people *will* understand, and they will be the best friends you've ever had in your life.

You are not up a creek without a paddle. The paddle is sitting right beside you. All you have to do is reach down and pick it up.

Shannon

RECOVERY WORKSHOP

If I had a penny (oh, heck, a dollar) for every e-mail I have gotten over the years from someone bemoaning their unlucky fate at contracting an eating disorder . . . well, let's just say it seems we all react equally poorly to our diagnosis—at least at first. However, over time, I have learned that there is one defining line that sets the survivors apart from the rest. The survivors understand that *everybody has something.*

Alcoholism. Abuse. Anxiety. Alzheimer's. Cancer. Depression. Dyslexia. Divorce. Drug addiction. Grief. Loneliness. Poverty. Anorexia. Bulimia. Binge eating disorder. EDNOS.

The list is endless. If you are a Christian, maybe you call it your "cross to bear." For Hindus, it is your karma coming back to haunt you. For Buddhists, perhaps it is just another worldly desire in need of renouncing. For the rest . . . well, call it what you will, but to my eyes it is simply the universal human condition.

Like it or not, admit to it or not, accept it or not, this is the way life is. And I won't attempt to trivialize what we each go through by saying that "life is hard." We all know that all too well by now. But what is less known is that above, inside, behind, and beyond the struggle lies the real truth worthy of recognition, which is that life is also *wonderful*. And it is only when we tap into the universality of our struggles that we can finally access our own allotted portion of that wonder.

Your assignment for this Workshop is to watch the rap artist Eminem's cinematic biography, *8 Mile*. As you watch, contemplate this statement: "From the *opposition* of great adversity comes the *opportunity* for great triumph."

Pay close attention to early scenes where the audience and the other rappers mock Eminem for his dreams. Imagine that their words personify the voice of your eating disorder, and that his initial responses personify how you have been reacting to your eating disorder's taunts. Then, later on, watch what happens as Eminem changes his responses to their derision and unbelief, and how that affects his dreams of success. Now, imagine yourself doing the same.

If you must have a reputation, what better than to be known as an overcomer? No longer a victim, but strong, powerful, wise. No longer an object of pity and scorn to yourself and others, but an icon of respect, a conquering hero returning to your hometown in victory. And if you must have friends, what better than to cultivate friends who are just like you—victorious fighters!

In many cases, we are the company we keep. When we keep company with our eating disorder, we become our eating disorder. When we keep company with our fears of being discovered as the human beings we are, we become somewhat less than human. When we keep company with those who do not wish to push through their own obstacles or support others who do, we become small, afraid, and weak. However, when we keep company with other heroes, with pioneers who persevere to carve out a path for themselves when none is easily seen, *we become a hero as well.*

Take your own walk down 8 Mile. And, when you reach the culmination of your journey, pause for one final satisfying moment to turn around into the glorious sunset and wave a conquering hero's "good-bye" to your eating disorder—forever.

Life Celebration Affirmation:

A snow-white rapper in an all-black business . . . could any conceivable endeavor hold any less likelihood for success? Eminem's passion for his craft, for self-expression, for contributing what he has to share, has changed the face of rap music for all who come behind him.

Your passion contains the same explosive power. Audiences from all walks of life are able to relate to Eminem's movie because of his *story*, regardless of his ethnicity, gender, or background. Likewise, as you meet, accept, and respect your own story in progress, your power to change your life and the lives of those who follow hopefully in your footsteps will ignite, light, and transform the path of recovery for us all.

During the sometimes grueling but always fruitful days in between, affirm without fail to yourself these or similar words:

My one shot is here. Opportunity is knocking and I will answer the door! Look—see—I am opening the door. I am walking through it. I am taking by force of will my chance to heal, to live, to climb on the back of my eating disorder, to reach up and grasp hold of my very real birthright and legacy—reclaiming my life through lasting recovery!

The Last Samurai

Shannon—

I am getting so sick of fighting. I realize my four years is practically nothing compared to some, but it's nearly a fourth of my life. I'm sick of waking up every morning only to be faced with the same challenges and failures that await me each day. I make the same mistakes unconsciously, without even realizing I'm making them. Then it hits me, and I think, *Oh crap, I screwed up, oh well, better luck next time,* only to repeat the cycle over and over and over again. I don't know if I've ever told you, but I am almost a brown belt in Shotokan karate. We sparred a lot during class, and I really like that kind of fighting so much better than what I'm going through right now. It is clear-cut. You hit, you score a point. You miss, they score a point. When eight points are scored, the set is over (at least in Shotokan). I'm good at that kind of fighting. I can use weapons, I can defend myself. I'm pretty much a bad ass, at least when it comes to karate. But this. I am so sick of the mental fighting. Mental fights are so much harder to win.

Michelle

Hi Michelle –

Regardless of where the battleground is currently located, it is still a contest of wills where the opponents are evenly matched, and may the best (wo)man win. Here is an opportunity to use your outer skills in karate to mentally visualize the inner battleground. Call on all the moves that you know are effective, and use them against your opponent, the eating disorder. Do not give up until you are standing alone in the ring. Do not ever make the mistake of underestimating your opponent or of turning your back on it. You must stand, ever vigilant, face to face with your eating disorder, and fight.

Shannon

RECOVERY WORKSHOP

Whether we are aware of it on a daily basis or not, we all have so many battles under our belt that we have already fought and won. And yet, in the face of a challenge dauntingly called "recovery," we observe ourselves with shock as we spinelessly cringe and cower and wimp out—often before the real fight has even begun! Who is this person with their hands over their eyes, whining like a baby? No—it couldn't be—that couldn't possibly be *me*!

So, what is it, exactly, that is so intimidating about recovery? Why do we allow our own minds to psych ourselves out right at the critical mass moment, time and time again?

For this Workshop, your assignment is to watch the movie *The Last Samurai* starring Tom Cruise. Pay careful attention to the condition Cruise's character is in when the movie begins and to what causes his eventual transformation into a samurai warrior without equal. Notice the approach the samurai warriors and their families take toward each day of life and each task. Ask yourself how you can, following the way of the samurai, discipline your mind to focus at each moment on your goals—and *only* your goals—for recovery.

Here is the bottom line. And it is the same for each of us—for Michelle, for me, for you:

RECOVERY IS NOT OPTIONAL.

It simply isn't. Without recovery, we will all die of our eating disorder. This is a fact. Eating disorders are lethal. Fatal. Heartless. All-consuming. The moment you forget this fact is the moment when your mind will begin to waver, and your recovery will crumble.

For extra credit, take a few moments and read through the story below. I heard this parable several years ago while living in India, and I have never forgotten it. As you read it, imagine that you are the man in the story. Ask yourself how you can apply the king's wisdom to your own recovery.

King Janaka's Secret

A man is seeking spiritual enlightenment. He has heard of a famous and unimaginably wealthy king named Janaka who supposedly possesses the secret to finding peace in life. This man, not having any inner peace of his own, wants desperately to learn how King Janaka has found it and how he can find it for himself. He decides to travel as a supplicant to Janaka's kingdom to ask for more information. The man comes into the town on the day of the kingdom's annual celebration—as he arrives the entire community is out partying in the streets! He walks through the center of town, makes his way through the milling crowds and up to the palace gates, and when he finally kneels before King Janaka, he humbly begs the king to tell him the secret of peace in life. The king instead says, "Did you see that big party happening all around you on your way to my palace?"

"Yes I did," the man replies.

"Well," King Janaka replies, "I order you to walk back through the center of town carrying a bowl of water on your head. If *one drop* spills from that bowl while you are walking, the guard walking behind you will chop off your head."

The man was shaken, to say the least. He didn't expect this—he didn't want to die just yet. But what could he do? The king had spoken! So he put the bowl of water on his head and walked back out the palace doors and through the center of town, carefully balancing it on his head. He looked not to the right nor to the left; his complete concentration was on making sure that the precariously placed bowl of water did not spill. When he got back to the palace, King Janaka asked him, "Did you notice the spinning jesters, the fire-eaters, the sweets vendors, the entertainers, the bands?"

The man said, "No, King, I only was aware of the bowl on my head, and of making sure it didn't spill one drop."

The King said, "That is how I have found peace in the midst of my plenty. I wake up every day and look at my life and realize that any hour could be the hour of my own death, and in this way I don't get attached to anything I have, nor desire anything I do not have."

In the same way, begin to train your mind to replace any thoughts of recovery being *too hard* or *impossible* or *not worth it* with only one single refrain: *recovery is not optional.* Awaken the samurai within. And vanquish the opponent in your path, once and for all.

Life Celebration Affirmation:

You have a steadiness within you that you have not properly appreciated, until now. The same slow and steady progress that has sustained the development of your eating disorder all these months or years is the same path you must follow to attain sustained recovery. And I must tell you, no case could have looked more hopeless than my own, staring straight into the mouth of an enemy I could not name for seven long years. Yet here I am today. I am a samurai.

You are a samurai. So, the next time you are tempted to forget who you truly are in the face of some lesser force posturing to gain your attention, affirm instead these or similar words:

I have the heart, mind, and spirit of a warrior. I am charged on my life to protect the sanctity and honor of the palace within which I dwell—my very own body. And I accept this charge willingly, proudly. I will fight to the death to protect it from marauding armies, inner mutinies, the lies of spies, and the machinations of an eating disorder greedy to obtain for itself what I have and hold. My enemies will never take me or what is mine alive—and I will live to see the day of my eating disorder's demise!

Catch Me If You Can

Dear Shannon—

I remember one of the doctors at treatment coming up to me after a team consult and sharing with me that no one had any concerns whatsoever regarding my determination and will toward recovery. That they all knew that I was going to be one of the ones that "made it"—they had no doubts. Part of me was pleased with that affirmation, but mostly I thought, "Wow! All these prominent eating disorder specialists, and I've fooled them too. I am GOOD at this!"

I am ashamed. Have I been lying to you too? Have I allowed you to think that I'm strong and walking in the right direction?

Nadia

Hi Nadia—

You have several choices today. You can choose to believe me and your doctors. Or, you can choose to say, "Those doctors, Shannon, they don't really know me. I know who I am—and I am *not* that person they describe who is courageous in her recovery efforts."

Those are your two choices. And each day as you wake up you get to make the choice again.

Shannon

RECOVERY WORKSHOP

I remember the day I came face to face with it—with *it*. With "the choice," the heartbreaking choice. I realized I was still living, still doing my recovery work even, as if I could somehow have both. I was still behaving like I could somehow keep my eating disorder *and* recover from it too. This was the child in me, the little girl who didn't understand the very adult concept of choices and their consequences.

Similarly, I have met countless individuals with eating disorders who, in a desperate but fruitless attempt to cling to both their life and their eating disorder, are still trying to explain their circumstances away as something else. Their eating disorder is a figment of someone else's imagination. It isn't really an eating disorder at all—it is Lyme disease, cancer, food allergies, a thyroid imbalance, depression. And, if it is, in fact, an eating disorder, at the very least, it is far less serious than their family/husband/wife/treatment team/best friend/child has been making it out to be—why is everyone else always overreacting? Their recovery is paper-thin, and, inexplicably, in the face of their ever-weakening state, they are spending precious reserves of time and energy trying to fool those around them into thinking they are getting better.

For this Workshop, your assignment is to watch the based-on-a-true-story movie *Catch Me If You Can*, starring Leonardo DiCaprio and Tom Hanks. Visualize yourself in Leonardo's role, with all of the unique challenges and unavoidable changes he is confronted with, and then study how he initially chooses to handle those challenges and changes. Ask yourself how you can relate to his story, his need to meet the (real or perceived) expectations of others, his desire to please. Watch him as he runs away from the very real issues in his life to impersonate an airline captain again and again . . . and how he responds when he lets another human being, played by Tom Hanks, get close enough to offer him a new approach to handling life's challenges, and a chance to turn over a new leaf—this time with a true and compassionate friend standing by his side.

Pay especially close attention to the scene near the end of the film when Leonardo's character, Frank, lets down his guard and finds himself once more turning to his old coping patterns for comfort. But this time, Carl, played by Tom Hanks, pursues him. Carl catches Frank just as he is about to board the plane, and says, "I'm gonna let you fly tonight, Frank. I'm not even going to try to stop you, because I know you'll be back on Monday." To which Frank replies, "Yeah? How do you know I'll come back?" Carl's reply is short and to the point. "Look, Frank, nobody's chasing you."

Stop the movie and ask yourself how you have been spending your misdirected potential—your intelligence, drive, ambition, creativity, and perfectionism. Have you been perfecting the art of running away, of dying? Because, if you choose to die, you will be

very good at dying. But, if you choose to live—well, guess what—
you will find that you are equally good at saving your own life.

It is time to shift your awareness and intention daily toward living; swing the loaded cannon of all that misdirected potential around, point it at your eating disorder, and fire away.

Life Celebration Affirmation:

Choosing well involves a process of preparation. First, the question must be asked and then answered: "Am I worth it?"

The answer, by the way, is always "Yes."

But sometimes our mind still needs convincing. Sometimes we spend so much time and effort trying to convince those around us of something so we can avoid admitting to ourselves that we are the only one who remains unconvinced.

So, now, begin to fertilize the field of your mind to welcome and support this new blossoming of truth by affirming these or similar words:

I deserve to make good choices for myself, and I can choose well. I have no need to run anymore. I have the power, the confidence, and the ability to stop, turn around, and make the best choice in any given situation, without hesitation. I have already proven to myself that I have everything I need to recover—well and fully—from my eating disorder. I have intelligence, drive, ambition, and creativity in spades—and I now put it to very good use as I powerfully reclaim my one and only precious life!

Donnie Brasco

Hi Shannon—

I struggle with food every day. I fight the voices that tell me, "Don't eat that" and "Look how fat you are," but as soon as it gets a foothold, it takes over like it has now. I hide it by eating small but healthy portions when I'm around people in situations where eating is the focus, but even then I don't keep it down. It feels like poison in my body and I have to get rid of it or stay away from it.

In the past, it got to the point where the things the eating disorder voice would tell me were my thoughts too, like, "No one really thinks you're a pretty person, look how fat you are, don't eat that it's going to make you fat, but if you do eat it you can always throw it up." I thought that I was really the one in control, and that what I was doing was normal and completely healthy. I didn't know where my thoughts stopped and the eating disorder's started. I guess in a lot of ways I still don't.

Jenna

Jenna—

So now it is time to explore what you really mean when you say "I feel fat."

You have to begin to decode the meaning of the messages the eating disorder voice is conveying to you; you have to crack its little code. You have to learn to speak its secret language.

Shannon

RECOVERY WORKSHOP

Scientists and mathematicians say that math is the only universal language. Musicians claim the only language that needs no translation is music.

But for those of us with eating disorders, it is quite clear—the only language that is truly universal, and worth learning, is the language of fat.

In the movie *Donnie Brasco*, one of my favorite mob films, we learn how members of the Mafia can, to unsuspecting ears, color the phrase "Forget about it" to mean anything from compliments for a great dinner to a verbal death sentence.

Sound familiar?

In the same way, we must teach ourselves to decipher the many subtle shades of our own meanings for the word "fat."

For your assignment, watch the movie *Donnie Brasco*, paying particular attention to the characters' use of the phrase "Forget about it." As you watch, think of all the different situations where you are tempted to say "I feel fat," and try to figure out your true meaning for the phrase in each situation. Here are some techniques to help you get started:

1. Every time you use the phrase "I feel fat," notice what happened just before you uttered it. Who was there? What was the topic of conversation? For this first part of our exercise, you are not yet trying to make any sense out of what is occurring when you feel "fat." You are just *noticing* the "what, who, when, where" that is co-occurring at the moment when your fat feelings first begin to arise. You are also looking for patterns. Are certain people often or always present when you feel fat? Do you feel fatter in certain situations than in others? Do certain topics of conversation trigger fat feelings more readily than other topics? Just observe the ebb and flow of "feeling fat" in your daily life—as an objective, curious reporter who is going to report back to you later on her findings.

2. Divide a piece of paper into six columns. Label each column with the name of one of the six primary emotions: happiness, surprise, fear, anger, sadness, disgust. Then, under each heading, write synonyms for each—for instance, are you feeling sad or are you grieving? Is that really sadness at all, or could it perhaps be anger? Are you enraged, indignant, or, possibly, intolerant or even resistant? This step challenges you to expand your emotional vocabulary as far beyond "fat" as possible. The more different, *accurate* ways you have to describe the shifts in your emotional landscape, the less likely you will

be in moments of stress to label your *feelings* as fat. The bottom line, as my friend and colleague Jess Weiner likes to say, is that "Fat is *not* a feeling!" So, in applying this exercise to your daily life, go under the same premise—that, whatever you are feeling, it is not fat. Once you know this, you are free to discover what you are really feeling, and what that feeling has to teach you about strengthening your recovery.

3. Divide a piece of paper into two columns. On one side, write "I feel fat." On the other side, write "Which really means . . ." Decode the real meaning behind the phrase in relation to your response to different situations, and, in this way, defuse the ticking time bomb inside you. So with this third part of our exercise, you are using your list of adjectives to correctly identify and then name each emotion. When I did this in my own recovery work, I felt so incredibly empowered. Knowledge really *is* power—newfound power you hold over your eating disorder to make choices that lead toward lasting recovery! So use the knowledge you have learned from these exercises and continue to be vigilant in the days to come about noticing, identifying, and naming your real feelings.

4. Pay attention to the quality of the inner voice that has been so faithfully reporting your "fat" feelings to you. Does the voice sound familiar? Could it, perhaps, be the same voice your mom speaks to you in when she is upset with you? Could it be your teacher's or your family physician's voice? Or maybe it is the voices of the bullies in school? Here we are separating out *your* voice from the voices your eating

disorder uses to get your attention. For example, my eating disorder would, at various times, sound like many voices from my past and present who were unkind or harsh to me, or voices who in the past had sounded sweet, but only for the sake of manipulating me so that I would do what they wanted me to do. Sometimes my eating disorder would talk to me like my music teachers, or my math teachers (they were never very pleased with my scores). Sometimes it would use the tone of disappointment my parents had when I had not lived up to their expectations. It took a long time before I was able to separate the eating disorder voice from my own, but eventually I learned how. Here is the telltale difference between the voices—the difference that this exercise is beginning to help you discern: *Your* voice—your true voice—is always *genuinely* compassionate and kind. Your real inner voice always gives you the benefit of the doubt and a chance to learn and grow from areas in your life that are distressing to you. Identifying the voice of "fat," the voice of the eating disorder, in whatever way it attacks you, clearly separates this other voice from your own, and returns to you the right to work through your own recovery with compassion and self-respect—imperfectly, one day at a time, just like the rest of us, and at the pace that is right for you.

5. Also, begin to notice how the voice speaks to you. Where is it coming from—from what region of your body, from in front of or behind you? And when do you hear the most messages—when does the voice get the loudest? When you're

doing well or when you're doing poorly? When you're achieving or when you're so-called "failing"? Does it speak before you have had a success or a failure, or after, or both? Here, we will begin to evaluate all the information you have been gathering in the previous exercises. You now have identified patterns—interactions, places, times when you are more troubled by "feeling fat." You have been able to put names to many of the feelings you formerly, automatically labeled as "feeling fat." Your ears are starting to hear the eating disorder voice underneath its masquerades as other, more familiar voices, so you can tell not only when you are being attacked, but also who your true attacker is.

Now, in this exercise, you will begin to get a sense of how pervasive the eating disorder voice's influence is over your life. Are you hearing it all the time—*even* when there is nothing going on, no one around you, no reason to worry and maybe even every cause to celebrate? I got to a point where the eating disorder spoke to me at every moment, in every hour of every day. I was never allowed a moment's peace. At this point, I began to realize how invalid the eating disorder voice's comments were and how pointless it was to listen to anything it had to say. I realized none of its commentary was helpful, accurate, or based in reality, because *even if* it did have something of value to say, I could not hear it through the emotional paralysis caused by its alternately vicious or poisonously kind tones.

6. Create a new voice—a voice that speaks softly, is strong, can

kill the ED voice with genuine kindness and human compassion, and is always waiting in the wings to help you get
back up again when the meanness or manipulation within
has driven you down to your knees. Finally, in this conclud-
ing exercise, you will begin to make the choice to no longer
give the eating disorder voice any airtime at all. You have
knowledge. You have power. You have awareness. What do
you do with it? How do you use it to change the level of
influence the eating disorder voice has over your life? So
think of someone in your past or present who has always
spoken to you with genuine kindness. If no one immediately
comes to mind, think of a movie character or a song with
encouraging lyrics, or just imagine you have a new puppy or
kitten and consider how you would speak to your new pet
as you orient it to its new life with you. *This* voice—this sin-
cerely kind, quiet, reassuring, empathizing voice—is the
voice you will be listening to for direction and support from
here forward. You may have to literally create the voice from
scratch, using your imagination about how you would like to
be treated (*not* how you think you deserve to be treated or
how the eating disorder voice tells you that you deserve to
be treated) or how you would treat someone else who was
suffering like you are.

It will take some work to listen for this voice underneath
the manipulations of the eating disorder voice. And again,
take good care as well not to mistake the "kindness" of the
eating disorder voice for this new voice—the eating disorder

is not above killing with its own brand of "kindness." You can identify your new voice not only by its tone but by the quality of its messages and instructions. If the voice is encouraging you to work *toward* your recovery goals, you are listening to your new voice. If the voice is encouraging you to work *against* your recovery goals, then you know which voice it is, and you can practice your newfound skills in ignoring it.

We have spent significant time on these exercises. This is because it was one of the critical mass areas for me in beginning to wrest power back from my eating disorder. There is an enemy working against you from the inside out. In these six exercises, you have been learning the lay of your enemy's territory, studying how it moves about in your mind and your life, noticing where it likes to hide and then leap out at you when it thinks you are at your most defenseless. You are like a good spy, studying the mob boss, learning his killing secrets, so that you can catch him in the act and save innocent lives—in this case, your own!

Life Celebration Affirmation:

For most of us, removing the word "fat" from our vocabulary can be one of the first major steps we take to make room for putting the word "life" back in! Each time you are tempted to or actually catch yourself thinking or saying "I feel fat," stop yourself immediately and affirm these or similar words instead:

I feel. I can feel. I have the capacity and the right to feel when I am sad, when I am happy, and every feeling in between. "Fat" is not a feeling, and it is not good enough for the new me—the me who craves the fullness of life the way a bird craves bigger, stronger wings to fly ever higher. I don't have to settle for "fat" anymore. I know better. I deserve better. I am better. I give myself safe passage through each page of the dictionary, the thesaurus, and my own heart, until I find the absolute perfect word to describe how I am really feeling in each situation. And then I honor myself by feeling it!

The Mirror Has Two Faces

Hi Shannon—

I remember when I was fourteen years old I began to feel like I just didn't fit in anywhere. My mom pulled me out of school in sixth grade and started homeschooling me because of bullies at school. I was too short and too smart to be a "cool" kid. My personal view on my body has never been good and that just makes it worse. I can't remember a time when I haven't felt like the most unattractive person in the room.

Jenna

Hi Jenna—

I know it's hard to do this work, to rally enough to even make the attempt, when you feel worthless, ugly, unlovable, and all those feelings I also used to feel. But you must try. When I first started to heal, my motivation had nothing to do with feeling worthy of it. But I saw there were other people around me, fat people, thin people, rich people, poor people, old people, young people—who lived with much more happiness and joy than I did. So I started to believe it was possible for me to change too and be more like them—happier, more alive.

Shannon

RECOVERY WORKSHOP

The Dove Campaign for Real Beauty (launched in 2004) surveyed over three thousand women worldwide between the ages of eighteen and sixty-four. Only 2 percent of women reported a willingness to describe themselves as "beautiful"—even though respondents stated that "physical attractiveness is about how one looks, whereas beauty includes much more of who a person is." In addition, the women affirmed that they regarded as "powerful components of beauty" a combination of attributes that include "happiness, kindness, confidence, dignity, and humor." Yet one in four survey participants confirmed that they have considered using plastic surgery to enhance their beauty! (For more on the Dove Campaign for Real Beauty survey results: http://www.campaign forrealbeauty.com/uploadedfiles/dove_white_paper_final.pdf)

Clearly, the international consensus is that beauty is a holistic, multisensory *experience* that is seen, heard, felt, and sensed with every faculty at our disposal—and it is *not* fundamentally body-driven. However, it is equally clear that, as with recovery, it takes time to discover and experience beauty in ourselves. In tandem with our rate of recovery progress, beauty unfolds within and expresses itself progressively to us on four distinct levels—physical, mental, emotional, and spiritual.

Case in point: Have you ever met a person who, at first, appeared to your physical eyes to be absolutely drop-dead gorgeous? But then later, when you met her and interacted, somehow her attractiveness faded? Conversely, have you ever met someone who initially had a less alluring physical presentation, but, after even just a short conversation, you suddenly discovered that you couldn't take your eyes off of her?

Welcome to one of my all-time favorite principles of lasting recovery: Whole Wo/man Beauty.

Before we dive into the assignment for this Workshop, I invite you to do a little prep work. The next time you are out and about, pay particular attention to the people around you. Look at couples, parents with children, families, friends chatting over coffee, and ask yourself what draws them together. Is it purely their physical presentation, or does it go much deeper than that? Is it always those with bodies that appear to conform to today's media-driven beauty standards who have the smiles on their faces? If you went out into your local community and tried to prove that "thin is the new happy," would you find enough evidence amongst your neighbors to support your claim? Journal about your findings.

Now, for your four-part assignment:

1. Watch the movie *The Mirror Has Two Faces*, starring Barbra Streisand and Jeff Bridges. Journal your thoughts about these pivotal points in the storyline:

a. Why did Barbra's character choose to undergo such an extreme external makeover?

b. How (if at all) did her outer transformation affect her ability to experience the loving relationships in her life? Did her outer makeover conform to her expectations of how it would change her experiences of loving and being loved?

c. Given that Barbra herself produced and starred in *The Mirror Has Two Faces*, what do you think motivated the notoriously choosy star to tackle this particular topic? (Hint: Read *The New York Times* interview with Barbra for insights—http://query.nytimes.com/gst/fullpage. html?res=9B0CE2DC113BF930A25752C1A960958260)

2. Journal about the characteristics Barbra's husband, played by Jeff Bridges, cited that made Barbra so beautiful to him. Then rank them in the order of importance to him *as stated by him* in seeking a continued relationship with her.

3. Think of three wo/men who inspire you to keep fighting for recovery. For each, describe in your journal what qualities make each of these particular wo/men such a beautiful beacon of hope for you.

4. In your journal, divide a page into four columns. Label them: physical beauty, mental beauty, emotional beauty, and spiritual beauty. Write down five ways you can cultivate beauty for each aspect of you. (Note: For the segment on "physical beauty," all ideas must be free from reliance on

eating-disordered thoughts and behaviors—i.e., no mention of weight management, numbers on a scale, measurements, or comparisons).

In *The Mirror Has Two Faces*, we learn that, regardless of how limited *our* perception of our own beauty may have become, others can see and experience our beauty on multiple levels and in many wonderful ways. Wouldn't it be fantastic if we could experience our own beauty in these other ways as well! The movie also teaches us that our limited concept of our own beauty—especially when we persist in reducing it to pertain to our physical appearance alone—limits not how others perceive our beauty, but how much we are willing to allow others to get close enough to us to show us that our beauty goes way beyond skin-deep.

Our work thus becomes, not just in this particular exercise but in each day of our lives, to move our concept of beauty within. We can do this by allowing others to connect with us and to share with us how they perceive our beauty, as Barbra finally allows her husband to do for her in the movie. We can also do this by asking ourselves how we are showing and sharing beauty on spiritual, mental, and emotional levels and by being willing to experience for ourselves our Whole Wo/man Beauty!

Beauty—*real* beauty—is so much more than what lies on the surface of your skin. And so are you!

Life Celebration Affirmation:

When leading fashion magazines run advertisements offering financing for plastic surgery to any woman who wants it, it is easy to forget that we have more to offer than what we see in the mirror. But we do. We are so much more than we can ever comprehend by staring at our physical reflection.

It is time to meet the rest of us. It is time to experience our own beauty from every angle. So the next time the silvery glint of a nearby mirror beckons, close your eyes, turn within, and quietly, powerfully affirm these or similar words:

The mirror may have only two faces, but I am a multidimensional being. I exist, breathe, and live physically, mentally, emotionally, and spiritually. I have a beating heart within me that animates my face, my limbs, my form. I have a radiant mind that pierces through the flat numbness that has characterized my former obsession with my disease. As a newly emergent star recalls its blackrock beginnings, so, too, I remember my days when "thin equals happy equals me." But my firm heartbeat and steadfast mind now shine through that predictably unchanging darkness to light my way. I am wo/man. I am whole. And I am beautiful.

The Man in the Iron Mask

Hi Shannon –

I spent my childhood having it drilled into me that there was only *one* right way, and it wasn't mine to decide. That you *don't* talk, you don't share private things, it's wrong, it's bad. And then, you get this therapy stuff where you are told that the exact opposite is true. And it makes sense, mostly, except it's so ingrained in you and you feel wrong and bad to even *want* to tell. I have found that this is when I need someone else to be the grown-up for me for a little while. I am a rule follower, and somehow it doesn't seem like as much of a betrayal of the past if I am just following somebody else's rules now. I think that's why it's so hard for me sometimes to accept the responsibility of "getting" to choose how things are going to affect me. I know I need to, but I'm just not ready. I wouldn't go back to being a kid for *anything*, yet I missed out on a lot, didn't I? I never learned how to grow up in some ways. And I became very old, very fast, in others.

So when I got your e-mail and you are "telling" me things to do—answer this question, write more often, etc.—well, there is such a peace in that! I can't allow myself to think it's okay without permission, but there's now a certain sense of freedom! Is your head spinning? Mine is. I don't want to die, Shannon, I guess I just don't necessarily want to live all the time, either. Not like this. And I am forced to speak. I would be a good prisoner, I think. Nobody would be able to get things out of me that I thought might hurt or jeopardize someone else, whether they were right or wrong. I guess I kind of am a prisoner, aren't I? I allow myself to be, I guess.

Nadia

Hi Nadia—

No, I don't believe you would be a good prisoner at all. How do I know? Because a "good" prisoner doesn't *look for a way out*! You might be a resigned prisoner or even at times a willing prisoner because you are so aware of the pros and cons of your situation, but you are not a good prisoner. You rail against the boundaries and restrictions of your life—Nadia, you are *mad*! Your anger is fueled by a lifetime of fear and silent disagreement with those around you whom you perceive to have had a stronger voice than you do and more of a right to use it. And your anger won't go away if you just silently hide out in your self-imposed cage—in fact, it will grow.

Shannon

RECOVERY WORKSHOP

In Nadia's letter, one fundamental misunderstanding leaps out into plain view: the erroneous belief that, just because we're in prison, we are somehow suited to the lifestyle.

None of us dreamed of spending our lives in the prison of an eating disorder when we were born. And yet so many of us wake up every day, keys in hand, and walk straight back into the prison of our own making to lock ourselves in again. Why?

I can tell you that one reason I had for doing that in my own life was that I felt safe in there! It was known in there. *I* was known in there. Some of us have languished in prison for so long that we could recreate in our minds every bar or brick or stone of our cells, both hatefully and lovingly all at the same time. We know our prison, walls, bricks, and bars, better than we know ourselves.

Your assignment for this Recovery Workshop is twofold:

First, watch the movie *The Shawshank Redemption* starring Tim Robbins and Morgan Freeman. Pay particular attention to what happens when the lifetime prisoners are released, and make notes about how each handles their newfound freedom. If you were handed the opportunity for total freedom from your eating disorder today, would you be ready, willing, able? Why or why not?

Next, watch the movie *The Man in the Iron Mask* starring Leonardo DiCaprio. Keep your journal close by and chronicle how Leonardo's character, Philippe, reacts to two critical experiences— to the initial removal of the iron mask, and to his evil twin brother's subsequent attempt to lock him back into the mask again.

After watching both films, ask yourself these questions:

1. What are the benefits to staying in prison?
2. What are the benefits of breaking out of prison into freedom?
3. Do you believe that freedom is something you can have and hold?
4. What will it take for you to be able to accept and maintain your own freedom from your eating disorder?

I have often heard it said that when the pain of staying stuck becomes greater than the pain of trying something new, that is when breakthroughs come. Whatever your reasons for continuing to choose to live in prison when you have already won parole, understand this: you signed your own parole papers the day you chose recovery, but only you have the power to choose to *live* your hard-won and wonderful life of freedom!

So, right now, before you think another thought, speak another word, or lose your nerve—get up from your hard stone bench, put one foot in front of the other until you have reached the end of the hall, open the heavy prison doors, and *walk through them* to greet the wide blue sky.

Life Celebration Affirmation:

We need our prisons more than they need us. We need all of the benefits we have decided that only prison can provide us. Understand this: the cage will not mourn when we walk away. Its empty steel bars will not weep for our absence. Neither will the cell dissolve through lack of use—it will simply sit, for the balance of our lifetime, waiting for us to return. It will neither rage nor cry. It *will* seductively whisper to us during our weaker moments, "Hey, remember me? You used to shelter here. You used to call me 'home.' You used to trust me. I am still here for you—come back, come back."

In these moments, when our very normal human needs for comfort and security arise, we may find ourselves listening to the whispers of prisons past as they beckon us back into their cold, steely arms. In those moments, it is up to us to wake up quickly and affirm these or similar words:

I can take care of myself. I can. I was born with the ability to meet all of my human needs in safe, healthy, and appropriate ways. If I do not know how, who, when, or where to appropriately meet my needs, I can ask. I can ask trusted others for help. I can turn to my support team. I can call close friends and confide in them. I can turn to myself and journal my questions until answers come. I can safely and confidently wake up each morning and stop myself from returning to my cold stone prison—no matter what the new day brings. I have the wisdom, the power, the good judgment, the will, the perseverance, the determination, and the right to set myself free. And I will set myself free—I am even now setting myself free!

The Curse of the Black Pearl

Hi Shannon—

Aww, things are just not right. Can I ask you some questions? Things are really tough right now. I'm so tired of being tired, of wishing away my days. I feel like I just don't care about anything or anyone anymore, but I must care at least a little bit or it wouldn't bother me, right? We just got back from our first family vacation ever, and it was nice but unsettling. I mean, here I am, lying on a beach looking at a beautiful sunset surrounded by my family, nothing to worry about, and I couldn't help but think, "Wow, if this doesn't make me feel something, what in the world will?"

I want to care enough to do something—I *think* I care enough to do something—but I just don't know what it is. Do you remember these feelings? I hope you never had them because they are terrible, yet at the same time I guess I wish you did because that would mean that I'm not as crazy or as alone as I feel.

Nadia

Dear Nadia—

The most reassuring thing I can say is that dry periods happen, but they don't last. I think you may also be mourning the loss of some habits you had grown to rely on. You are making huge strides—to the point where you can actively perceive how "wrong" right feels—and now it is such a huge change that it is shutting you down. You feel dead because all of a sudden you want to feel *alive!* So take heart. Don't be afraid of your dryness … let it be what it is for now, temporary but still real, and with its own necessary purpose for being.

Shannon

RECOVERY WORKSHOP

I have always loved the scientific principle that nature abhors a vacuum. I find comfort in thinking that, before we can be filled up with good things, we must first create space in our lives for the good we desire to pour in. For instance, for so long we have been consumed by, filled by, obsessed with, and focused upon the demands and discipline of our eating disorder. So, when we view recovery from a different perspective, that of releasing and relinquishing our eating disorder in favor of the rest of what life has to offer, it becomes easy to see that *before new good can come in, there must be an emptying-out of the old bad that takes place.*

This explains the dry spells that sometimes occur. When we reach the point in our efforts to heal where we have exhumed and disposed of a significant number of old, damaging behaviors and habits, we must then be strong enough to live with the emptiness that remains for a time. At this critical juncture, we must challenge ourselves to turn our attention not to worrying that our efforts have been for nothing but instead to visualizing and drawing to ourselves the long-awaited, healthier preferences and visions that have been driving our healing work all this time.

This is what is known as "Good Drought." These are the times when we must be extra vigilant to notice not just the "what" of what is happening but the "why" of the bigger picture lurking just behind it. For this reason, for this Workshop, your assignment is twofold:

1. First, watch the movie *Pirates of the Caribbean: The Curse of the Black Pearl* starring Johnny Depp. Pay special attention to the cursed pirate crew's longing for the curse to lift so that they might be able to feel and enjoy life again.

2. Second, imagine you are a cursed pirate, longing with everything in you for the curse to lift even for one moment so you can taste an apple, feel the warmth of the sunshine, cool off in the rain, and feel your own heartbeat. Create a list of all the experiences you can recall when you felt like life was worth living, when you were glad to be alive—then continue by listing the experiences you haven't had yet that you still long for. Refer to this list when the emptiness looms, and you need something reassuring—something besides your eating disorder—to cling to.

Finally, remember this—for every cycle of Good Drought, as in every other phase of recovery, there is no way out except through. There is no way out except through.

There is no other way out except through.

So grab your courage in both hands, and walk on through to the other side, where your very own wonderful, rich, and full life is waiting to welcome you!

Life Celebration Affirmation:

For me, the most difficult phase of the Good Drought cycle has always been what I call the "not-caring." You know what I mean—when you lack even the weakest sense of motivation to lift a finger to help yourself—or to harm yourself for that matter. It is the closest experience of the "walking dead" that a living human being can ever have—more profound in its effect than even an eating disorder could ever be, because at least with the eating disorder we are consumed with *something*. In stark contrast, the all-consuming nothingness of Good Drought often threatens to eat its own hopeless, feeling-less hole through our soul.

So, during these periodically necessary tests of endurance and patience, I have often found it helpful to repeat these or similar words:

Nothing that is truly meant for me can ever be taken away. And nothing that is not truly meant for me can remain. I embrace what comes to me and willingly release what goes from me, in acceptance of something even bigger and better that is on its way. I do not need to feel or "do" my way to discovering myself. I can simply take comfort in the evidence of my being-ness, as seen through my own eyes. I am patient. I am kind. I am strong. I am love embodied, and love conquers all—even the "black hole" of the Good Drought times in my recovery life. I trust myself to stay the course, leaning on my growing ability to accept each ever-evolving phase of life without resistance or struggle, always focused on the valuable lessons each phase brings. I trust and lean on the stories of others who have emerged from times like these—victorious, joyful, and grateful. I trust. I survive. I believe. I wait patiently and expectantly day-by-day for the wonderful and fulfilling life that is even now coming to occupy the welcoming empty spaces my eating disorder is leaving behind.

Spring, Summer, Fall, Winter . . . and Spring

Hi Shannon—

I've dropped the ball big time since we "spoke" last. I just lost it. I've basically spent the last five days playing Russian roulette (actually eeny, meeny, miney, mo; don't laugh at me!) with Vicodin, laxatives, cigarettes, wine, caffeine pills, scissors, and a scale. My weight has dropped, my stomach aches, my head is pounding, my teeth hurt, and I just plain blew it. I hate this stupid disease or whatever it is. I hate it, I hate it, I hate it. And I don't even care that I sound like a spoiled little brat, because that's exactly how I feel and I am going to *let* myself feel that way! So there! Stupid disease.

Nadia

Nadia—

Flirting with our self-destructive side is something every one of us has done from time to time. But don't turn it into a love affair. This challenge you face now is all of our individual challenge in this lifetime: to overcome the dark loneliness we run from and learn to keep good company with ourselves, all by ourselves, and to learn to do it with safety, integrity, honesty, and grace with ourselves and others.

I do know exactly how you feel right now, but I also know it can be just another season in the flow of your life, *if* you will allow it to pass on in favor of something new and better that is up ahead.

Shannon

RECOVERY WORKSHOP

We will always be tempted to approach our recovery work with the same linear, black-or-white thinking that has served our eating-disordered mind so well in keeping us locked in a vicious, if simplistic, battle with inches and pounds. We are either doing "well" or "poorly." Life is either "good" or "bad." We alternately deem ourselves "ill" or "healthy," "fat" or "thin," "hopeful" or "hopeless." We will either long for life or death. We are used to alternately giving our all to our recovery work or self-destructing with similar single-mindedness.

But our recovery progress cannot be so neatly confined—in fact, in order for it to work, it must necessarily take the opposite approach and function in our lives as an *integrated*, holistic process. At every moment, we are continually healing, growing, transforming, evolving—and not only physically, but mentally, emotionally, and spiritually as well!

A few years ago, I watched an independent film that cast a spotlight on how this really works. The film was called *Spring, Sum-*

mer, Fall, Winter . . . and Spring. It chronicled the life of a young monk-in-training and his teacher. The elder monk, along with his young protégé, lived in a simple little hut where he also worked as a healer, and families from all around the region would bring the incurably sick to him for miraculous restoration.

Over the course of the film, the backdrop of seasons changes with the seasons of the impetuous and impatient young monk's life, as he meets a girl, falls in love, commits a crime, serves his sentence, and eventually returns to the hut of his master to finally emerge from his trials and challenges no longer in training for life, but a full-fledged master himself.

For your assignment for this Workshop, as you watch the movie, contemplate how this is playing out right now in your own life and recovery work. Ask yourself where you may have been resisting or rushing the process, impatient to move on when the lesson is only half-learned.

One of the most important understandings to take from this exercise is this: *seasons happen.*

It may sound overly simplistic, but it is in simplicity that we often find some of our greatest strength to endure and persevere. This awareness gives us the kind of natural structure that can replace our need for the artificial structure that our reliance on the instructions of the eating disorder has been providing for so long.

In time, just like our body clocks become regulated to the shifts from dawn to twilight, our recovery clocks will become fine-tuned to pick up subtle seasonal shifts that will help us prepare, withstand, and eventually even enjoy what is on the horizon for us!

Life Celebration Affirmation:

A few months ago I came across a wonderful saying in a popular magazine: "Courage is fear that has said its prayers."

Repeating this saying to myself, which I have done often since I first read it, reminds me that feeling fear is a normal expression of growth. It is normal to want to cling to the known, even when the known is threatening our noses, fingers, toes, or hearts with frostbite or third-degree burns. I always remind myself that experiencing my own courage is not first vacuuming out all vestiges of terror and *then* fearlessly moving forward, but instead involves harnessing the adrenaline-energy of my fear *now* and using that energy to propel me forward.

So when you are buffeted about by the high winds of arctic winter or the heat waves of scorching summer and fear holds you paralyzed in place for more of the same, encourage yourself with these or similar words:

Courage is fear that has said its prayers. As one door closes, another bigger and better door opens even wider and beckons me to enter. One season always gives way to another—I can trust in the ebb and flow of nature what I am only now learning to trust in myself. I hold my destiny in the palm of my wide-open hand, and my fear is only more proof that I have what it takes to courageously break free from the extremes of arctic winter and scorching summer into the gentle, seasonal flow of recovered life.

Something's Gotta Give

Dear Shannon—

I've not been doing well lately, I know I've not. Call it excuses, call it whatever, but I have just gotten so sick and tired of trying and failing, trying and failing. Could I be trying harder? Absolutely, I'm sure I could. I'm not trying to blame anyone or anything except myself, but I just got *done* [with treatment], you know? Tired of going to appointments, talking about yucky things, paying zillions of dollars, tired of thinking all the time and wondering and worrying . . . so anyway, things have happened over here and I took them maybe in a way that I shouldn't have, but I guess I kind of made a commitment to, well, "recover in my failure," so to speak. Just maybe the lessons that I was brought here to teach are ones that I will only be able to teach after I die. I know, I know, don't say it, but you know what? Once I started feeling that way, there was such a peace to me, one that I have missed for a very long time. So last week I started to share some of this with my therapist—not all of it, but enough to let her know that I didn't think I would be coming back.

I am not sure what is going to happen with all this, but *something* is. Because, you know, part of me doesn't want to quit. But it just can't keep being like it's been. So that's it. All I've got! I'm not sure what is happening now or what the future will bring. This is the best "cry for help," I think, that I've got in me right now. I believe it's selfish of me, but I also feel that I am being more honest and open with the people in my life than I have ever been. I want to do right.

Nadia

Dearest Nadia—

You haven't dropped the ball. I personally believe you are *picking up* the ball for the first time ever in your life. This is what real life looks like, Nadia. Saying, "Screw you, I'm going my own way—you figure it out." Making decisions, even if the decision doesn't look so good to you or to those around you (which is all in your perspective anyway and can change the moment you decide to change it). Taking a stand for what you will and will not submit to. Sharing your life with caring friends and mentors and telling the truth even if the truth doesn't agree with "old Nadia" who just wanted all the waters of life to run smooth and polite. You are doing it at last. You are being *healthily* selfish—taking care of *you* for the good of you and all concerned.

Shannon

RECOVERY WORKSHOP

The word *controversial* comes to mind when I reread correspondence with Nadia from this particular time in her recovery journey. Advising or encouraging anyone to discontinue treatment or therapy sessions is treading on dangerous ground indeed.

So I will say up front, especially for those of you who may be reading my words to Nadia while preparing to dance the Snoopy dance of victory, hold up. The point of this Workshop is not to let you off the hook of doing the hard work of healing, for as long as it takes to heal. The point of this Workshop, instead, is to identify if and when therapy may begin to, even if only temporarily as in Nadia's case, *interfere* with the business of getting back to living, which is really what all of your hard recovery work is for!

Sometimes, when we are stuck, it is important to keep pressing forward (think boot camp here). And it may even be that all that is needed is to sit down, have an honest conversation with your treatment team members, share your sincere frustrations, reservations, or fatigue around continuing to do the hard work of recovery, or continuing to do it the same way you have grown accustomed to doing it, and then together, you can brainstorm ways to breathe new life into your treatment program so that you can continue to enthusiastically participate.

But sometimes, what is needed most is to let go and try something new. (Again, you may be able to accomplish this through a simple reassessment, or it may be time to try even more creative approaches that can allow you to continue your progress in recovery.)

For this reason, your assignment for this Workshop is a three-parter:

1. Watch the movie *Something's Gotta Give* starring Jack Nicholson. As you watch, pay attention to the evolution in Nicholson's character as he begins to comprehend that the behaviors and habits he has clung to for support for so long create such a restrictive structure that there is no room within them for him to *live*.

2. Make a list of areas in your recovery work where you are feeling stuck, stifled, de-energized, bored, frustrated, angry, or even hopeless—where, in short, you keep feeling like something's gotta give or you just don't know what will happen next. Think also of longer-term issues you have been working on where you just can't seem to make that all-important breakthrough.

3. For each of the "red flag" areas you have identified above, write down to the best of your recollection what you have been doing to achieve results in these areas and the length of time you have been trying to make progress. Then, ask yourself these two questions: (1) What were your expectations when you began work on these issues?, and (2) Where are you now, relative to the time and effort you have spent working on these issues, in relation to where you want and hope to be?

And if you, like Nadia, run into a situation where you truly, in your gut of guts and heart of hearts, believe that the best and only route to success is a complete break from the current structure of your daily therapeutic routine, then discuss it with your treatment team and create, as best you can, a safety net of supportive people who can be on call for you if you happen to need them during your rest period. Then trust, and let go.

Maybe you might even delightfully wake up the next day to find yourself to be in surprisingly good hands—*your own!*

Life Celebration Affirmation:

Self-trust is trust's Pearl of Great Price. It is the hardest won and the most meaningful—it is the holy grail of all trust-related journeys and the source out of which all other trust springs.

Unsurprisingly, it is also a journey few of us successfully complete. This is because self-trust takes practice, just like any other skill worth developing. We earn our own trust by not pushing ourselves too far, too fast. We also take care to exercise self-compassion—there is a reasonable and an unreasonable level of fear, and we do not throw ourselves off the end of the pier before we first say to ourselves, "Okay, I am ready." We take a step back, pat our own back, hold our own hand, and ask ourselves, "Is today the day? Or do you need to wait a few days more?" Then we listen for our own answer, and respect our own feedback regardless of what our answer may be.

So, as you begin this process of learning self-trust, affirm these or similar words for yourself:

Trust does not grow on trees—trust is grown on the tree of my life as I take small, daily steps out of my comfort zone, holding my own hand for reassurance and support. I too can live an amazing life. I too can be my own best friend. I too can have the adventure of a lifetime at my own side. I too can safely and wisely choose the relationships, situations, and experiences that are best for me, and boldly say "no" when I mean no, and "yes" when I mean yes. I am strong; I am a fighter and a survivor. I am worthy of my own trust.

28 Days

Shannon—

Hi, I just got back from treatment. I was gone for over sixty days. It is so strange to be home. Treatment was a transforming experience. I am home and feel so different and yet here everything is the same. Sadly, same place, same feelings. I had hoped that the urges that had subsided in treatment would be less strong here. Unfortunately, ED is rearing its ugly head and wanting more of me again. However, I am more in control this time around, and I am trying to use the skills I learned in treatment and reach out for support before I make choices that will lead me down an ugly path.

I had planned to go to my support group tonight, but the reason that I have not gone yet is more than a little juvenile. I just feel so huge. I still have a problem comparing myself to everyone and feeling a longing to go backwards whenever I see someone very thin, or when I accidentally or, worse, actually choose to look at myself in the mirror! It is very scary and has a way of squashing my efforts that day.

Krista

Hi Krista—

I am sure it is strange to be back. Be patient with yourself. Be kind to yourself. Managing the small stuff is not small right now—it is huge. Do well with the little challenges in your day and they will add up to the point where the bigger challenges can pretty much take care of themselves. You must look at recovery as a cumulative series of baby steps that gather in power and strength over time.

Shannon

RECOVERY WORKSHOP

In its own toxic, deadly way, the eating disorder has been the best of friends to you. It has been your shelter when you were too overwhelmed to function. It has been faithful—always waiting by your side to comfort you when others let you down. It has made sweet promises that, however illusory, have filled your weary heart with hope at just the right moments. It has promised to always tell you the truth—even if it has never delivered on its promise.

And this means that, like with any other significant love and loss relationship, you simply must grieve for what you are giving up, before you can move on to gain your life back again!

There is a scene in *28 Days*, one of my favorite movies, where Sandra Bullock's character, Gwen, meets her new therapist for the first time. She has been convicted of drunk driving and is serving twenty-eight days of court-ordered rehab in lieu of jail time. In their initial meeting, her therapist wastes no time but gets right to the heart of the matter—Gwen has a problem, and it needs fixing. She doesn't take the news well. Subsequent sessions yield similar results, and, after one such session, as she storms toward the door, her therapist cheerily bids her farewell with a common recovery saying, "Just take it easy and keep it simple!"

She turns around and fixes him with a baleful glare as she retorts, "I am so tired by the way you people talk, you know, I mean—one day at a time, what is that? I mean, like, two, three days at a time is an option?"

One day at a time is all we get. And, to be honest, that is more than enough to keep us busy.

Your assignment for this Workshop is a two-parter. You will use *28 Days* as your guide.

1. As you watch the film, journal about how Sandra's character's recovery work mirrors the five stages of grief (as outlined by Elisabeth Kübler-Ross in her book *On Death and Dying*):

   a. Denial: "It can't be happening."
   b. Anger: "Why *me*? It's not fair!"
   c. Bargaining: "Just let me live to see . . ."
   d. Depression: "I'm so sad; why bother with anything?"
   e. Acceptance: "It's going to be okay."

2. Journal about where *you* currently are in your recovery process as related to the five stages of grief. See where you may have tried to skip ahead prematurely, and go back to complete any work that remains undone. Use this model

to inject a note of patience and perspective into even the roughest of days. (Note: Keep in mind that it is normal to "skip around" while progressing through the five stages of grief. For instance, you may find that one day you feel depressed, the next day you have a moment of clarity where you feel accepting of the outcome, and then the very next day—or moment—anger may arise, and so on. The value of the grief process is to keep cycling through until you achieve an experience of ever-increasing sustained *acceptance*. Patience with the grief process, as with recovery itself, is key here.)

Grief, more than anything else, is about *honoring* your feelings—even just feeling your feelings is not enough. Whether you are grieving over a choice that was made for you or a choice that you have made, you have feelings about it, and you deserve to feel them! This is the part where the honor lives—in recognizing your right to feel your feelings and experience them free from judgment—even your own.

There are so many reasons why we as human beings resist the grief process—we are afraid, we think it will hurt too much (and it may, but that does not mean we will not survive it), we think we don't deserve to grieve, we think there is no need to grieve. . . . The list is almost endless. Yet the fact remains that we get *nowhere* in our recovery work until we accept the role that grief can play in either keeping us stuck or moving us forward. Becoming willing to grieve for a loss—without judging it or hanging on to it—is the *ultimate* act of courage. As you witness yourself moving through each stage of the grief process, you will awaken a sense of honor and heroism within yourself that you had no idea was there.

If you can allow yourself to truly and fully grieve the loss of your eating disorder, giving full honor and respect to what it has given to you without negating all that it has taken from you—if you can do this—then you will know beyond a shadow of a doubt that you also do have the power to *let it go!*

Life Celebration Affirmation:

Into every month a little rain must fall, and a little progress must sprout. Sometimes we do not call it progress. Sometimes we do not see it that way. But every day, with every step along the way, we are learning. Even if it is just one more reconfirmation of what we already know, we become that much the stronger for it.

A year seems so much shorter when broken down into twelve-month increments. A month seems so much more manageable when we remember that it holds (at most) thirty-one days. So, for at least the next twenty-eight to thirty-one days, and longer if necessary, remember to daily affirm these or similar words:

I am learning. I am growing. I am transforming, even when I do not believe myself to be. I, like all other sentient life, cannot help but evolve (thank goodness). Yes, an eating disorder has happened to me. I tried being angry about it, but anger sapped my strength and got me nowhere. I tried bargaining to keep it, and got sicker for my reward. I even tried to just give up and die, but I found to my credit that it wasn't in my nature. Now, it is time to grieve, to acknowledge the good with the bad, to be thankful for what this experience has taught me, and to face my eating disorder with profound respect as I say good-bye. Good-bye, ED. Thank you for what you have taught me about life, other people, and me. I am the better for it.

Girl, Interrupted

Shannon—

I just wanted to let you know that I am going into a treatment center tomorrow. I sort of had a blackout while driving yesterday and had an accident. I suppose it was the proverbial "straw that broke the camel's back."

Thank you for everything. Please keep in touch.

Krista

Dear Krista—

I am glad you are doing what it takes. Hang in there and *fight!*

Shannon

RECOVERY WORKSHOP

In those first years when I got sick, I spent a lot of time in the self-help section of our community library. I was searching—for somebody, for something I had no name for, for answers, for a clue that could lead me anywhere, to anyone who had ever felt like me.

I had already done the bulk of my healing work from anorexia and bulimia before I heard that there were places where people with eating disorders could go away to, staffed by people who were trained and willing to help them heal. I still remember the night I met a young woman who told me that she had just been discharged from a place called Remuda Ranch. "What is that?" I asked her.

Amazing. To think that, all those years while I struggled alone, there was a place I might have gone to where I could have found the help and support I was searching for! Such a priceless opportunity. And yet, how many of us truly recognize such priceless opportunities when they come along and take full advantage of them?

Your assignment for this Workshop is to watch the based-on-a-true-story movie *Girl, Interrupted* starring Winona Ryder.

Imagine that you are the person Winona's character is based upon. Imagine that you have (essentially) loving family members who possess the resources, courage, and willingness to get you the help you need. Pretend that you have a team of treatment professionals who want nothing more than to see you heal and who believe you have what it takes to get better. Imagine also that you have a group of individuals you keep company with while in treatment—some of whom want to get better and some who do not.

Then, ask yourself this one question—given all this, what will be the single determining factor that will predict the outcome of your recovery?

In the movie, Winona's character, Susanna, goes from fighting her treatment team and aligning herself with the troublemakers, to fighting back against her illness and siding with those who have her true best interests at heart. Her choice ultimately makes all the difference in the world in her own life.

The same holds true for you. Every month, I am contacted by at least one person who tells me a story that spans back years—tales of inpatient treatment stays and subsequent relapses. The point of the letter is usually the same—treatment just "doesn't work."

Just because you go to treatment or get sent there by someone who cares doesn't mean you are going to get better. It is *still* your choice. You must seize hold of that chance with both hands, hang on for dear life, and fight for your right to live. Even if the treatment center is not a perfect fit for your needs, there is still something of value for you there, something that has the potential to move you closer to your recovery goals *if* you are willing to persevere to find it.

In my own recovery journey, I have discovered that anything worth having—anything lasting—will most likely not come quietly on its own. You will have to fight for it, be willing to spend a lifetime to achieve it, try again and again and again to attain it, before you will finally grow strong enough to hold onto it for good.

So if you do have the chance to obtain treatment at any level, make the most of it. Remember why you are there. Learn from any desire you may uncover to rebel against the treatment professionals who are there for the sole purpose of helping you get better, or any similar desire you discover to befriend those who do not want recovery over those who do and are willing to work for it. Recognize your fear wherever it is at work, and work *with* your team to root out that fear and replace it with courage, determination, and healing.

Ultimately, an eating disorder is just an educational interruption in your "regularly scheduled programming," which, of course, is the unfolding of your own wonderful, worthwhile life. Keep this understanding at the forefront of your awareness, and, while you are undergoing treatment, set your body, mind, heart, and spirit to do the very thing your eating disorder tells you that you cannot do . . . because you *can!*

Life Celebration Affirmation:

Treatment is hard, yes. But then again, so is life. The simple truth is, if you have managed to survive having an eating disorder, then you certainly have what it takes to recover from one! Old habits die hard, including the habit to fight to hold onto what is trying to kill you. Learning new habits starts the same way that you learned the old ones—with repetition and reinforcement, in your mind.

So, each day while you are recovering, do not fail to affirm these or similar words:

I will not tolerate this interruption for one second longer than I need to in order to master the lesson it holds for me. I am here to learn, to grow, to love—not to die from an eating disorder! I have my own anthem of triumph to sing, and I will not stop until my lone voice of victory resounds around the world to proclaim, "Yes, I can!" Whoever wants to join me on my quest, come on. You are welcome here. I am grateful for your help and will be your most diligent student and willing partner as we work together to end this interruption once and for all and resume the regularly scheduled programming of my life.

Last Holiday

Dear Shannon—

I spent my day in the hospital yesterday. I passed out walking between classes. I was very dehydrated, so they just hooked me up to an IV for about an hour and a half and sent me home, but it was no fun. The past few days have been especially tough. I'm not really sure why, but I've been struggling even more than usual. Sleeping has become pretty much nonexistent and the doctor said he will not put me on anything unless I stay at the hospital because he is afraid that I will take too many, and I don't have anyone that can monitor my meds. So I just don't sleep.

It's interesting to me how you said that your music [singing and playing] was what kept you going and that it was the only thing that kept you from suicide because it's exactly where I am. "No," the logical part of my mind says, "You don't really want to die," but then the suicidal thoughts get hold of me and it scares me really bad.

Jenna

Hi Jenna—

Don't run from the desire to consider death and its role in your life—what we ignore often only haunts us more. If you tamp down and refuse to think about death, you will miss discovering *why you are choosing life!* What will you miss if you weren't around anymore? What kind of life would make life really worth hanging on to?

Shannon

RECOVERY WORKSHOP

"Consider death." What does that mean, exactly? Is that morbid thinking? Should we, out of polite discretion at the very least, look the other way and pretend not to notice the socially uncouth piece of us that is constantly trying to starve, binge, or purge ourselves to death?

It is high time to admit to ourselves that, *yes*, we think about death. It is now an appropriate moment to concede the point that sometimes (and especially on our really bad days) the thought of death can even be comforting. And we are long, *long* overdue to comprehend the fact that if we wanted—*truly* desired—to kill ourselves, we would have *done it already*. It is simply imperative for us to admit that we are much less afraid of death than we are of never really learning how to live.

While I endured much at the hands of my own eating disorder in the years before I began my recovery work, I found it all tolerably manageable until the day the anorexia rendered me unable to play, write, and sing music. Victimized by this, the ultimate indignity, I suddenly wanted to kill myself. In the altered state of mind that my suicidal desires imposed upon me, my one remaining lucid thought became, "You know, Shannon, you can always kill yourself tomorrow. Before you do that—before you do that one thing which you know you cannot take back—is there anything *else* you would like to try first?"

In my answer to this insanely sane inquiry, I discovered the first real seeds of the hope I had been searching for. It shocked me to realize that yes, there really was something else I might like to try first. Several somethings, in fact.

Your assignment for this Workshop is in three parts:

1. Watch the movie *Last Holiday* starring Queen Latifah. Pay particular attention to how she initially reacts to the news of her prognosis. Then, notice how her reactions change as the "certainty" of her own demise gives her courage she never knew she had to embrace life.

2. Ask yourself what you would do if you were given a similar prognosis. Where would you go? Who would you visit? What would you do? Create your own "Book of Possibilities" and continue to add to it as often as ideas occur to you. (Hint: In my own recovery, I taught myself to instantly recall my "possibilities list" in the moments when my mood turned dark and I started to lose hope.)

3. After you have completed steps one and two, go back and rewatch the scene in the movie where Queen Latifah's

character is looking at herself in the mirror on New Year's Eve. Grab your journal and record your reactions to her statement: "Next time, we'll do things different. We will laugh more, love more, we'll see the world—we just won't be so afraid." What if you really could do it all over again—starting *now*?

Chances are good that we have lived so long in the grips of the nightmarish dream of "thin" that we have forgotten all of our good dreams—all the dreams that make life feel like it is worth living. So take yourself on a richly deserved, all-expenses-paid "Last Holiday"—and when you return, prepare to celebrate by waving good-bye and good riddance to your eating disorder and to the thoughts of death that only come out when you believe it is not possible to live a recovered life—because you can, and you will, and, even now, you are!

Life Celebration Affirmation:

Thinking about death—especially our own—keeps us honest. It keeps us brave. It keeps us asking the tough questions and searching for the tough answers—in short, it restores our integrity and self-respect, because we courageously come out of hiding to confront the real issues fueling our continued struggles with our eating disorder.

But it is not a destination—not now, not yet, and certainly *not* for something as potentially curable as an eating disorder. For now, for our purposes here in recovery, it is simply another curious tourist stop on our journey, a hypothetical exercise for our enlightenment and erudition—nothing less, nothing more.

So, in those moments when persistent, alluring thoughts of giving up the fight for life arise, it is critical to reassure and bolster yourself with these or similar words:

I have the kind of relationship with myself that allows for me to explore any topic safely, completely, honestly, and courageously. I hold nothing back from myself—oh, no, not anymore. Death is a part of life, and even as I mourn the death of my old beliefs, my old habits, and the old eating-disordered world I have clung to for so long, I also celebrate the restoration of new hope, new life, and a brave new world that I have earned my rightful place in. When there is no need to hide from myself, there remains no one and no thing to fear. And I am not afraid anymore, because I know that, underneath it all, I truly do want to live—and I will live! I do live! I am alive!

NOTE: If you find that you are experiencing thoughts of suicide, seek professional medical care immediately.

Contact

Shannon—

I don't know what to do to commit myself to recovery. On some level I really want to get better, but I don't know how to live without the anorexia. I feel trapped and alone, and I feel like no one can help me. It seems like it should be so simple to just eat. But it's not. Every bite is a struggle and I usually end up failing. I don't know what to do at this point, and I do want to do what is healthy for me, and I know that I am doing the wrong thing right now. I just hope I can fix it before I do too much damage.

Lori

Hi Lori—

Deciding to recover and going for it really is a simple process. It doesn't feel simple while you're in the midst of it, but that's part of the work you have to do with yourself—to remind yourself that it is simple. There are complex reasons for what you are going through, including a possible genetic component, but the cure is simple—employing your considerable intelligence and sensitivity *away* from maintaining and deepening your disease and *toward* healing and recovery.

Shannon

RECOVERY WORKSHOP

1990 marked the year when I first realized I had a life-threatening problem with food and needed help. Mercifully, the many difficult years that followed have blurred somewhat over time. But 1997 stands out as the year I made "contact."

Watching the movie *Contact*, starring one of my all-time favorite actresses, Jodie Foster, I listened in awe as she explained the simple scientific principle of Occam's Razor to her date, Matthew McConaughey (lucky girl!). This principle, she explained, basically states that, "All things being equal, the simplest explanation tends to be the right one."

It is tempting—oh, so tempting—to tell ourselves that we don't know what to do. It is deceptively complex, we think. It is *so* confusing—all the reasons, the behaviors, the choices, the fears!

It is not complicated. We know what to do. We know why we are the way that we are, and why we have chosen our eating disorder to cope (Hint: biology + sociology = ED). We understand that, on some level, we now manipulate food because food is passive and cannot say "no" to the manipulation—just as we could not say "no" to whatever manipulated our thoughts, emotions, and self-confidence in the years before the eating disorder began. We may not know all of these things consciously, but deep down, underneath the roiling waves on the surface of our minds, we know why. And we know what needs to be done.

Learning *how* to do what needs to be done is what takes time. This is why you must make contact with two simple principles that will help you to weather the often-stormy transition between letting go of your old negative coping skills and adopting new healthy coping patterns in your daily life.

Your assignment for this Workshop comes in two parts. First, watch the movie *Contact*. Pay particular attention to the simplicity of each of the two main character's goals, and how their simple and clear intentions help them to persevere and eventually triumph despite almost insurmountable obstacles and complications.

Next, you will need two pieces of cardboard and one thick felt-tip marker, whatever arts and crafts supplies you prefer in order to add your own personal touches, and supplies to hang the finished project.

On one piece of cardboard, write the first simple principle:

FAILURE = Not getting back up

On the second piece of cardboard, write the second simple principle:

SUCCESS = Getting back up

Hang the finished cardboard signs in any location where you typically find yourself falling prey to the complex arguments of the eating disorder—you might consider hanging the set in the kitchen (especially on the fridge!), in the bathroom, or by the mirror. You might also want to make more than one set of signs to post in additional triggering locations.

And remember, success equals getting back up. Period. The end. The only way you will ever fail is if you fall down and stay down. Once again, remember that the reasons are simple. The means are simple. The method is where you will spend most of your time and energy.

So make "contact" with your own potential to access the essential simplicity of recovery. Remind yourself that you have all the right answers, you know the right things to do, and you simply must be patient with yourself as you unlearn old, longstanding, damaging habits and replace them with your newly adopted, healthier choices.

Make contact with your own courage as you try, fall, get back up, and try, try again, until at last you stay standing for good!

Life Celebration Affirmation:

I love watching Ultimate Fighting. Sometimes a new fighter joins the ranks of the seasoned professionals, and when he first makes contact with one of them in the ring, he usually ends up hugging the side rails—or worse. But if he keeps getting back up, keeps on fighting, it is just a matter of time before his opponent's complicated strategies meet his own simple perseverance, and he wins his first match!

In the ring with your own opponent, the eating disorder, victory will be found first in your head. Visualize the eating disorder, lying on the mat, defeated and lifeless. Imagine yourself, arms high over your head in triumph. Whenever you need an extra burst of confidence, repeat these or similar words:

I am success. I embody success. I know this because every time I get knocked down, I get right back up again. No matter what strategies the eating disorder employs against me, I do not waver from my goal. And I will get there ... oh, I will get there. I have no doubts. Even now, I am getting there, and it is inevitable that I will triumph because I simply will not give up—ever!

A Beautiful Mind

Hey Shannon—

This is my problem: I can't be honest. I can't let people around me (especially my parents) know I'm having such a hard time. I have no doubt that I would have support if I asked for it, but I can't make myself ask. I still have yet to admit to my therapist that she is right that I still have an ED, nor do I care to. I just can't be honest with her. I just can't do it anymore.

This weekend was an especially hard one for me. We had to go out of town for the weekend, and being out of town for two days means that you have to eat out for six meals in a row. Talk about anxiety attacks. It is absolutely zero fun. I wish I could just relax and talk to the others and enjoy myself, but it can't happen.

Michelle

Hi Michelle—

I read your e-mails, and all I can hear from you is, "I can't, I can't, I can't." Reread them yourself as *you*, not the eating disorder mind, and you will see it too. You can't tell your parents. You can't eat. You can't be honest. You can't enjoy good company at a meal. You can't, you can't, you can't.

This is just another way of saying "I won't." You *can*, Michelle.

Only the strong survive this battle. So be strong.

And do the thing you think you cannot do—because you *can*.

Shannon

RECOVERY WORKSHOP

I am often asked what "recovery" means. The common assumption, from both outsiders and insiders alike, appears to be that recovery occurs when there is no further desire—ever—to engage in the eating-disordered thoughts and behaviors as a way to cope with life.

Nothing could be further from the truth.

There is a fine, but definitive, line separating an "I can't" from an "I won't." Sometimes, we can't. As in, "I can't make a tree grow from a lump of coal." "I can't cure world hunger by tomorrow." "I can't force my sister/wife/best friend to let her eating disorder go."

But, sometimes, we can. As in, "I can help a tree to grow from a tiny seed, in time." "I can do my part to cure world hunger, one day by one day." "I can force myself, steadily and with strong, sustained self-effort, to replace my current need for my eating-disordered coping patterns with other, more beneficial life-coping skills."

For this Workshop, your assignment is to watch my all-time favorite movie, *A Beautiful Mind*, starring Russell Crowe. *A*

Beautiful Mind is the true-life story of mathematician Dr. John Forbes Nash, Jr., his Nobel Prize–winning discoveries, and his epic battle with schizophrenia, which went undetected until his disease had effectively wreaked havoc with his marriage, career, and life. Dr. Nash and his wife, Alicia, received some devastating news when they were told by his doctors that his schizophrenia was incurable. This was the truth.

What they were not told—what they were left to their own devices to discover—was that having an incurable condition did not mean there was nothing they could do to minimize its impact. John knew he had a beautiful mind, a powerful mind. He knew what his mind had already accomplished in the field of mathematics and inferred from this "evidence" that he also held within him the power to decode the mysterious ways of his disease and reclaim his life again.

It wasn't easy for him. It wasn't painless. And it wasn't fast. But it was—is—*possible.*

Near the end of the film, after he has already made significant progress in his recovery, Dr. Nash is asked by a colleague what the current state of his mental health is and how he maintains it. He replies, "I still see things that are not here. I just choose not to acknowledge them. Like a diet of the mind—I choose not to indulge certain appetites, like my appetite for patterns." In approaching the management of his disease from this aspect, he refers to all that he stands to lose—his life, his wife, his family, his career—if he at any point weakens his hold on his life in favor of his disease.

So, as you watch the movie, your one and only assignment for this Workshop is to chronicle in your journal all of the ways you may be continuing to subtly or overtly say "I can't" to your recovery journey, and then to begin to replace them with "I can." You can even make two columns—in the first column, write the "I can't ..." statement, and then in the next column, write its opposite— the "I can ... "

In this way, the next time you are tempted to replace necessary but difficult action with a seemingly easier "I can't" statement, stop and think twice. Pull out your list. Find the "I can't" statement and replace it with an "I can."

Fight the fire of "I can't" with the water of "I can," and put the raging mental fire of your eating disorder out, once and for all.

Life Celebration Affirmation:

Every single one of us has days that feel impossible. We have days when "I can't" and "I won't" feel interchangeable and inextricable. They aren't. We can always surprise ourselves with our resilience, determination, and strength. I was watching a favorite TV program the other night, and one of the characters, an older, motherly woman, was talking to a younger man about honor. She told him that honor is nothing more nor less than refusing to accept less than you know you deserve and are worth.

So, every time you are tempted to listen to a voice from your present or your past that claims that "you can't" do something you need to do for yourself, tune it out and instead begin to listen to yourself as you reaffirm these or similar words:

I can. I have honor. I have courage. I have resilience. I am determination personified. I refuse to accept less than what—than all—I deserve, in and from my life. I refuse to accept the life of a refugee, cowering in fear of what the next hour or day will bring. Instead, I take charge of my responses. I take charge of my thoughts. I take charge of my choices. I take charge of my mental, emotional, and physical power to positively affect the outcome of each situation. I use my beautiful, powerful mind to win my life back from my eating disorder, and, day by day, I succeed. Just like John Nash, I fight for myself, my family, my dreams, my life. And every day that I survive one more day of recovering from an eating disorder, I am a hero, a champion, a role model, to myself and to so many others who need to know that, yes, we really can!

Part Four

ED ON MY MIND

So, now, following in John Nash's courageous footsteps, we will begin to put our own beautiful, powerful
minds to work *for* us, against our disease. In these final
chapters, I introduce some of the key techniques from my
own recovery work that proved strong enough to break
the hold my eating disorder had over my mind and my
life—forever.

Use them with care—and with courage.

Enemy to Ally

Hi Shannon—

Do you read *Harry Potter?* In *Harry Potter*, the characters have the ability to draw memories or thoughts out of their minds and place them into what is called a Pensieve, which then stores the memories and thoughts until the person wants to remember them. Before memories and thoughts are placed into the Pensieve, however, they linger as a silver substance in the air. If I had the ability to draw out my thoughts, I would beat them down to the ground and utterly and completely demolish them. Unfortunately, I don't have that ability, and that makes them all that much harder to defeat.

Michelle

Hi Michelle—

I like your analogy; however, unlike with the overt eating-disordered behaviors, it is not necessary, nor have I ever found it to be that effective, to attempt to beat the crap out of our thoughts. For one, that just ends up feeling like more of the same; there's already quite enough yelling and beating up going on in there, thank you very much. The last thing we need right now is more! This is especially important, because your thoughts are still a part of the inner you. So you are not actually pummeling your thoughts, even if you think you are. Instead, you are wailing away on *yourself*, adding insult to injury, and that is never effective. Instead, it is necessary to transform the thoughts into ones that will work for you rather than against you.

Shannon

RECOVERY WORKSHOP

Just for grins (okay, maybe for more than that) I would like you to repeat the following six phrases to yourself, pretending you believe in their absolute validity as you do so. When you have repeated all six, grab your journal and write down your predominant feelings, thoughts, or mood.

I am beautiful. I am wonderful. I am smart. I am capable. I am worth loving. I am worth fighting for.

Now, I would like you to repeat a new set of six phrases to yourself. Again, when you have repeated all six, write down your predominant feelings, thoughts, or mood.

I am ugly and fat. I am an embarrassment. I am stupid. I am incompetent. I am unworthy of love. I am not worth fighting for.

So, how did you feel after repeating the first set of six phrases? The second? Compare and contrast your inner states. This is the time to begin to realize that how we allow ourselves to talk to ourselves will create an inner environment that is either hospitable or hostile to our recovery.

In my own battle to overcome my eating disorder, there was one strategy that enabled me, almost single-handedly, to take down the eating disorder mind for good. I realized, after the first year or two of struggling to recover, that a portion of my powerful mind had staged a revolt, intent on seceding from the union. I needed to do something—*fast*—to put down the uprising within.

I needed to learn to turn my mind from my enemy into my ally.

I soon discovered this was not nearly so clear-cut as I might have liked. The revolting part of my mind was a slippery little sucker. It *liked* to play games with my head. It got its kicks from outsmarting me, actually promoting inner wrestling matches where it could sit on the sidelines, cheering for the opposition, taking bets, and watching me kick the sh** out of myself on a daily, sometimes hourly, basis. So I decided that for what I lacked in brute strength and volume, I must make up for in subtlety. I began to enforce three practices to counteract the effects of its actions:

1. I bought a couple of books on the nutritional value of food, and I forced my mind to digest these new, positive thoughts about food's benefits while I physically chewed and swallowed. (See "The F.E.A.R. Factor" for more on the mechanics of this process.) With repeated exposure, some of the new thoughts started to sink in. My mind started turning its considerable critical thinking skills to figuring out the best foods,

in the proper combinations, at appropriate portion sizes, to meet "our" nutritional goals. It started to congratulate itself, not for how well it was sabotaging my recovery efforts, but for how well it was facilitating them!

2. At mealtimes, whenever possible (the five days I was at work each week, eating lunch in the cafeteria with the same people I saw each day, was an excellent place for me to do this), I chose a person whom, to my eyes, ate regularly and healthily, to be my "food model."* I was still afraid to make food choices, and my eating disorder voice would attack me viciously when I tried to plan and eat meals, so I designated my food model—unbeknownst to her or anyone else—to teach me about reasonable, consistent portion sizes. In choosing my food model, I took into account only two criteria—(1) I chose a person I deeply admired for her heart, who inspired me to have the courage to choose recovery *actively* by eating, and (2) I chose a person that I knew well enough to know that she did not have an eating disorder, who was also a person whose weight had remained consistent during the time I knew her. Once I had chosen my food model, how this would work was as follows: I would go to the cafeteria for lunch around the same

---

* The "food model" approach that is described above can serve as a good starting point in learning to identify and respond appropriately to hunger/satiety cues that may have been masked or overridden by the effects of the eating disorder. But it is just a first step. The ideal approach to reconnect with healthy hunger/satiety cues is to work with your medical doctor and dietician/nutritionist to develop a customized daily nutritional plan that factors in your body's unique genetic makeup, appetite, metabolic, and nutrient intake needs. During this process, it can also be helpful to designate a known and friendly "food buddy" to actually take meals and snacks with. Your food buddy can provide much-needed companionship, reassurance, and stress relief before, during, and after mealtimes.

time each day, find my food model in the lunch line, and slip into line behind her. My self-assigned "stealth task" was to observe her meal choices, and then, whatever she put on her plate, I would also put on mine. The outcome was phenomenal. Food modeling contributed three things to my recovery efforts that I had previously been lacking: (1) it eased the burden of choosing what to eat for lunch each day because I assigned that responsibility to my food model; (2) it removed the full weight of loneliness during the act of eating lunch by "sharing" lunch with my food model; and (3) observing my food model routinely consuming her lunch each day and maintaining a consistent weight effectively and repeatedly reassured the inner, panicked me with the proof that what the eating disorder mind had been telling me (if I ate anything at all I would instantly gain weight) was false.

3. I taught myself to reparent my mind. Every time my thoughts worked themselves up into a rebellious rage, throwing down and acting out in every conceivable inappropriate way, I would gently take my mind by the hand and kneel down to look it in the eye, saying calmly, *No, I'm sorry, you cannot starve/binge/purge/panic/scream at me/depressively fantasize about suicide. But you can do any of these other five things* (see "Flavor of the Month" for more on identifying new healthy coping mechanisms) *and you can choose any of the five you like, or even all five!* After which my easily diverted mind would busy itself deciding which one it wanted to do first.

Assert your authority over your revolting mind. *Now*. Begin to replace all thoughts that encourage a return to eating-disordered behaviors with thoughts that encourage your mind to want to use your new healthy coping skills. In this way, begin to make good on your plans to relegate life with an eating disorder to your past, where it belongs.

Life Celebration *Affirmation:*

Right outside the window of my old office grew several tall rose bushes. During much of the winter season and most of each scorching Texas summer, they were reduced to unattractively shriveled, dead-looking stumps. It was easy to assume, and I so often almost did, that they had outlived their place in the garden. And yet, virtually overnight, at the first hint of a cool spring breeze, fluffy colorful blossoms would unfold once more!

Recovery is like this. All that used to contain life appears dried up, dead, gone the way of what came before it . . . and then, with just a little application of effort and focused positive thought . . . *bloom!* So, when you have convinced yourself that this is the best you can do, have, or achieve in recovery, instead, stop immediately and affirm these or similar words:

I have respect for a worthy adversary, but I will not let this lesser part of me have its way. I am beautiful. I still have life, light, beauty, waiting in the wings to burst forth into bloom! I am in charge, and, by God, I will find a way to win my mind over to my cause!

Priorities

Hey Shannon—

I came home from school yesterday and tried to drink some water or something, but I couldn't make myself do it. I couldn't eat, I couldn't drink, I couldn't swallow my meds ... it was terrible. So, here I am, the morning after, and I still can't do any of the aforementioned actions. I find myself wondering, "Well, where do I go from here? I can only live for so long without anything to drink ... what am I going to do? Am I headed right back down the path to where my eating disorder began?" I really hope I am not, but I am afraid I am. I really think that I will be okay once I'm away at school. I'm not sure why I think that, but I do. I dunno, maybe I'm just making myself believe what I want to believe about school in the fall. Maybe it will be so incredibly hard that I will do nothing but resort to ED behaviors, but I really don't intend on doing that.

But as we both know, that's not the nature of this disease. It's not something you can just stop whenever you want to. It's not something you plan on doing ... it just sort of takes you over before you realize it. I feel so utterly hopeless, helpless, and I don't even feel like fighting again. I know if I don't, though, well, we all know what the ultimate end is without recovery. I don't need to elaborate, do I? I don't want that to happen.

Michelle

Hi Michelle—

I honor you for being willing to confide in me when you know I am not going to tell your ED mind what it wants to hear. Now, having said that, I cannot tell you how many e-mails I get from young women who claim they cannot take time away from their studies to heal.

Life first. School second.

Period. The end.

You must stop telling yourself it will get better when you get to college. Let me tell you, I tried that one too—it is a lie. In less than three months I had come and gone—I lost my scholarship, lost all my credit hours, lost everything. Better to wait and do it right than to rush and endure it all crashing down around you. Anything lasting must be built from the foundation up, including a degree. You don't have that foundation right now.

Shannon

RECOVERY WORKSHOP

S uccessful recovery really boils down to an ability to prioritize well. Life has so much to offer—much of which often appears, from the outside in at least, to conflict with one another.

For this Workshop, your assignment is to prioritize the action items in your life in top-down, top-five order. What are the five things you most wish to accomplish or achieve in your life—your big hopes, dreams, goals? Which ones cannot wait another day/week/month/year? Which ones must wait, if the other(s) are to have any hope of seeing daylight?

So, get out your journal and number your page from one through five. Write down the five things.

Then, turn the paper over and renumber a new page from one through five. In the number one slot, write "Survive my eating disorder."

Then, rearrange the other four top items in priority order underneath.

Understand this: Your eating disorder is not going to go away quietly if you apply yourself more industriously in class. What will most likely occur instead is that, as the stress grows, so will your need for your eating disorder (and if, instead of college, you insist that you cannot take time out for recovery because of your job or your family or any other seemingly significant reason, then understand that the same applies to you).

What good is the best degree, or the best job, or the closest relationship in the world, if there is no one to wake up to it each day?

If what you claim to value most is getting in the way of who you are charged to value most, then what is the only right course of action?

Most of the time, we know when we are feeding ourselves a line of crap, especially if that's the only thing we are feeding ourselves on a regular basis! We know when we are being dangerously unrealistic, when we are avoiding the obvious obstacle in hopes that, once it senses the awkward place it puts us in, it will just give up and politely go away.

The eating disorder will not go away until we force it to. And the rest of our life is not free or willing to approach us until the coast is clear.

Priorities remind your mind of what you are living and fighting for. Get some. Then watch your eating disorder get gone—for good.

Life Celebration Affirmation:

When we place our significance in exterior appearances, accomplishments, or responsibilities, we linger on the fringes of our lives in frailty and fear. We are so dependent! We are craving something ... anything. Will something "good" happen to us today, this week, or this year, so we don't have to feel so worthless inside?

No matter what it is that we long for, it will never be enough on its own to fulfill our need for self-respect. Until we place our own health and well-being in the priority slot, we will never find more than the rough edges of our cravings and desires to keep us company.

So, in those moments when you are tempted to substitute your outer accomplishments for doing the right thing by your inner self, no matter how hard it is or how much it appears to cost you in the short-term, stop and affirm these or similar words instead:

My life is worth nothing if I am not around to live it. I will miss me when I'm gone—not what I did, not who I knew, not the paper hanging on the wall or the paycheck in the bank or the ring on my finger or whatever else it is that I have attached my sense of significance to, but me. Just me. My life is worth everything—it is the Pearl of Great Price, and I will not forget that. I am the Pearl of Great Price, and I choose to live, and choose accordingly.

Relapse Happens

Hi Shannon—

I know that things in life make an eating disorder more prevalent, and I have tried looking at my life from the outside in (if that makes sense) to try and analyze things that could possibly be causing, I guess, a relapse of something I don't feel strong enough to fight right now. I don't really know what to do. I haven't said anything to my family, but I think they are beginning to see the obvious visual signs like weight loss, wearing clothes that I haven't been able to wear for a while, things like that. I have put my family through so much with this that it hurts me to have to tell them that it has become a problem, although I know that all they will want to do is get me help.

Jenna

Hi Jenna—

"Relapse" doesn't always mean regression. Often, it actually indicates growth! Have you ever heard life described like layers of an onion—the layers look the same, but get smaller and smaller and finer and finer as you peel inward? They make you cry just as much; they feel pretty much the same under your fingers, but just because each layer looks alike doesn't mean that it is. Each layer is utterly unique; each has its own purpose for being there, for being part of the onion's protection against the world around it.

This is the true purpose of "relapse." It is highly unlikely that you have regressed to a previous layer of illness. More probably, you have simply found a new, deeper layer to work on, another layer to peel back as you get closer to the heart of the matter.

Shannon

RECOVERY WORKSHOP

Onions have never been my favorite food. Most other people seem to love them. But as for me, about the only time I can enjoy the sight, sound, and smell of a round, fat, juicy onion is when I'm chopping them—for inclusion in everyone else's meal and exclusion from my own. Where is the enjoyment in that, you might ask? Well, chopping an onion is about the only time I can cry freely and openly, and no one feels uncomfortable at the display or compelled by pity or morbid curiosity to ask me, "Why are you crying?" It is obvious. There is the onion, the cutting board, the knife.

One of my favorite quotes of all time is, "Failure is nothing but success trying to be born in a bigger way." Or, in other words: *relapse happens.*

And, if it does, or more likely *when* it does, there is *always a reason*.

Figuring out the reason for your relapse is like the necessary work a mother does when her newborn cries and she must stop whatever she is doing—immediately—to discern why. In this way, you must learn to approach your relapse periods with the exact same sense of immediacy and urgency, and with a continual eye toward what you still need to learn in order to make your own recovery a reliable, lasting experience.

In fact, I often liken recovery work to realigning the tires on my car. If the four wheels are not all facing in the same direction, it is impossible to move the car forward. The four "wheels" of recovery are physical, mental, emotional, and spiritual. The next time you experience a period of relapse, evaluate your health on each level, and look for areas where you still need to strengthen yourself before sustained recovery can occur. Then, work on those areas.

Physical: Are you sufficiently hydrated? Nourished? Rested? Have you been overexercising to the point of exhaustion? Or are you missing the natural mood elevation that regular exercise could offer you? Is refeeding (see "The F.E.A.R. Factor" for more on refeeding) causing temporary, albeit unpleasant physical symptoms that you wish to avoid by returning to old habits? How is your physical health overall?

Mental: Are you mentally strong enough to endure appropriate weight adjustment with the proper perspective? What other coping skills have you added to your toolkit to replace your need for the eating disorder? Are you employing those skills, or have you retreated to what feels easiest and most convenient? How closely are you monitoring your thoughts?

Emotional: How at ease do you feel in the presence of your own emotions? Can you identify each emotion as it arises? How do you react to the presence of emotions? Do you have a plan of action to categorize, address, and release each emotion, especially those that are troubling to you? Have you given yourself permission to have, name, and feel your own emotions?

Spiritual: How do you experience and describe yourself? Do you have a strong sense of yourself from the inside out, or do you still relate to yourself based entirely upon a number on the scale, an image in the mirror, or the perceptions and feedback of others? In other words, are you able to clearly separate "you"—your heart, healthy mind, spirit—from your sense of "your body" and your ED mind's opinions about your worth and right to be? Do you consciously relate to yourself as a physical-mental-emotional-spiritual being?

If approached with the willingness to see and seize the opportunity it presents, understanding the why behind your relapse is information your healthy mind can use against the part of you that wants to take the easy way out—again—by using your eating disorder to cope.

So learn to use your times of relapse as rocket fuel for recovery, and, with its help, blast yourself beyond the need for your eating disorder once and for all!

Life Celebration Affirmation:

Who amongst us hasn't watched the progression of a thunderstorm across the horizon, secretly allowing ourselves to sink luxuriously down into its ominous, silky-dark depths?

This is not the right response to the appearance of a relapse period in your recovery life. No, what a relapse period requires—demands—from you is actually ascension into the highest places within, consciously seeking out the spaces where the light shines piercingly brightly above the midnight clouds and the air is so thin that only your dreams can dwell there safely.

Only from these heights will you be able to accurately perceive where the storm has rolled in from, where it is headed, and how to calm it. So, in periods of tumultuously enlightening relapse, bolster your courage to persevere by affirming these or similar words:

 I am strong enough for this. If I weren't, this opportunity would never have come knocking. Lucky me! I have the chance of a lifetime to learn where my weakness yet lies and to strengthen myself so that this too shall pass ... never, ever to return. I was made for, born for, so much more than a life spent battling an eating disorder. And, with each relapse, and each rebound once more into recovery, I am well on my way to claiming my very real eating disorder–free and wonderful life!

Twenty-Twenty Hindsight

Hi Shannon—

Last week I had a major meltdown with my therapist. I've never had one of those before. I'm usually pretty good at tamping down the emotion. I've never read any statistics or anything, but I'm thinking that there are more people who commit suicide while in therapy than at any other time. Don't you think? I guess you have to have ups and downs as far as emotions go, but I almost wish it wasn't that way. I think that sometimes when you're absolutely miserable and then you talk yourself down it's not necessarily a good thing.

Hey! I'm learning, though. "My name is Nadia, and I am not fine."

Nadia

Hi Nadia—

I was glad to get your e-mail and hear how things are progressing with your healing process. Major meltdowns can be good things—I've had many of those over the years in my own recovery process, and they've always left me stronger in the end. I would be curious to see if that is, in fact, what you discover as well.

I think very few people go crazy once they get into therapy, but I suspect many people go crazy getting themselves there. Don't you think? It's all about perspective for me. When I think I'm in the middle of a hard time, all I have to do is look back and see how much harder it used to be. And the years before I found help . . . those were the darkest for me, because I was so alone, so silent, so scared.

Shannon

RECOVERY WORKSHOP

Most of the time, I am just living from day to day like the rest of us—doing my daily work, tackling my daily challenges. I have no conscious recollection, on an hourly or daily basis, of how sick and miserable I used to be and, conversely, how much better I'm doing and feeling now. As one of my best friends is fond of saying, "It's all relative."

By this I think she means that in order to really appreciate my recovery journey, I must turn around and look behind me and remember "old Shannon"—the Shannon who weighed many pounds less and dragged through her days under the bone-crushing twin weights of depression and anxiety. I have to remember the Shannon who didn't have any friends, let alone a best friend, to call in troubled times. I have to remember the Shannon who didn't even know that what she had was an eating disorder, and thus assumed she was just going to die—without being extended the simplest courtesy of knowing why.

Over the years I have come to realize that I have made the most progress in recovery when I have remembered to keep a big-picture perspective. I call this big-picture thinking "Twenty-Twenty Hindsight," and it has offered me a continual source of motivation and inspiration on days when my enthusiasm for or belief in my chances for recovery have flagged. Scientists have conducted research to show that our brains are not capable of thinking two thoughts at the same time. We can either think one thought or we can think another thought. Similarly, when we are focusing on just one area or one trouble spot in our life, we cannot at the same time perceive the big picture of our life . . . and the very authentic progress that we have made toward our recovery goals.

So, Twenty-Twenty Hindsight is a mental discipline by which we make a *conscious mental shift* from one perspective—our narrow fixation on a single problem, issue, feeling, or moment in time—to another perspective—the overarching trend(s) in our overall life experience to date (big-picture thinking). To do this, we first acknowledge, "Yes, something about my life feels difficult, depressing, hopeless, confusing, and so on, *at this particular moment in time*" (trouble-spot thinking). But we don't stay in that thought or in the feelings it brings up in us for very long. That's because, using Twenty-Twenty Hindsight, we switch from trouble-spot thinking to big-picture thinking. We examine the whole of our life for areas where we have been in much worse circumstances—such as in all the days before we decided to choose recovery—and use that awareness to encourage ourselves to keep fighting! It's all about perspective and putting our singular circumstances into a bigger, more relevant, and meaningful perspective. (And while it is not our focus here, it is worth noting that we can also use this technique to think of times when we have felt happier, more hopeful, more safe, and more secure than we do today, and use this remembrance to encourage ourselves to remember that, just because we are feeling down today, it doesn't mean we will feel that way every day.)

So, your assignment for this Workshop will be to create a Recovery Timeline for your own use. The Recovery Timeline is a tool to help you use Twenty-Twenty Hindsight in a positive way to facilitate your continued recovery, and creating it is as simple as remembering.

Here is what to do—grab your journal or, if you prefer, a larger blank piece of paper. Draw a line down the center of the page, and at the very top, write the year you were born. Starting with birth, jot down the significant events and dates that contributed to the rise of your eating disorder. Put a star by the date(s) when you feel your eating disorder truly began, and again by the date(s) when you feel your disease has been at its worst.

After you have marked these dates on your timeline, write down anything you can recall about what your life was like *before* your eating disorder first arose—how did you feel, what were your thoughts, how did you spend your time, what was your experience of being in your own skin like? Next, in the time period that stretches from when your eating disorder first began to the present moment, note each date where you can remember making any progress at all in recovery. Try to recall how long each period was—an hour, a day, a week, a month, a year—that you achieved some small or great victory over your eating disorder. How did it feel—how did it make you feel—to achieve even the briefest triumphant release from your eating disorder's clutches?

Whenever you are having a hard time keeping to your recovery goals, look at your timeline and remember the time before your eating disorder began, and/or the times during which your eating disorder took an "intermission" from being a major player in your life and what that felt like. Know that if you have felt like that before, then you have all the proof you need that you can feel like that again one day.

Twenty-Twenty Hindsight reminds your mind of the bigger picture and refuses to let it—or you—believe that life with an eating disorder is all you will ever know. Do not hesitate to use your Recovery Timeline like the North Star it is—to guide you far and away from the black hole where your eating disorder patiently and eternally lies in wait for you, and toward the sunlight of recovery dawning on the not-so-distant horizon ahead.

As the sun's powerful rays begin to warm your face, your hands, your heart, do not be surprised to hear your own voice calmly say to your eating disorder, "Been there. Done that. *Never again*."

Life Celebration Affirmation:

We have Twenty-Twenty Hindsight for a reason, but it doesn't help us at all until we learn to read its signposts to guide ourselves away from the danger of the eating disorder and toward the safety of recovery.

So, the next time you catch yourself using your old eating-disordered thoughts and behaviors to cope with new situations, repeat these or similar words to yourself:

I somehow survived my past to get this far, which is how I know that I do have it in me to navigate the unknown path before me with great success. I affirm myself for paying attention to the extensive and valuable information my past provides to me, and for my willingness to look at where I have been—without judgment, but with compassionate awareness—so that I may learn and grow. I am grateful for my past, because it is my greatest teacher—in remembrance of what hasn't worked before, I am freed to discover what will work now, and I courageously employ these new strategies with great enjoyment and success.

The "New You"

Hi Shannon—

I don't know much about you and your personal struggle. Did it just "go away," or do you continue to fight it on a daily basis? I remember hearing you say when you came to speak to us at treatment that you had locked your keys in the car and your first thought was, "My salad's in there! I'm not eating responsibly!" And I remember being so uncomfortable with that because, to me, I'm either eating or I'm not—I'm healthy or I'm not. And yes, sure I have a struggle to go through, but once I take a certain final step it will be over and an eating disorder won't be a part of my life ever again.

Nadia

Hi Nadia—

In regards to whether the eating disorder just "went away" at some point in my own recovery process, no, it didn't. I will always have residuals of the fifteen years I devoted to getting "better" at being anorexic and bulimic. Those are old, familiar tapes, and it doesn't take much for the "play" button to get triggered again.

Shannon

RECOVERY WORKSHOP

For years as my recovery progressed I lived with this nagging feeling inside me—that there was another me, a "new me," trapped underneath the eating disorder who was totally different, better, more courageous, more successful, the life of the party, and a superstar to boot. There was only one problem—she couldn't get out. Like a genie locked in a bottle, this new me struggled against her confinement, weeping in frustration as she watched the so-called "real me" (aka the person who had learned so well how to live life through her eating disorder's voice and eyes) continue to make a big mess of everything.

Every time I would falter in my recovery, I would get so frustrated with myself—until one day I finally realized that the real me simply wasn't *ready* for the new me. The new me was too great, too cool, too wonderful to really be *me now*. I was still too invested in the identity I had built up of the real me, the me who was mirthless, worthless, powerless, hopeless, and helpless in the grips of my eating disorder. This was why, even as I entered the process of transforming into this new me that I dreamed of becoming—a me who was a much more confident, healthy, self-loving, and radiant version of myself—I often didn't see myself that way. It took quite some time for my past perception of myself to catch up with the new reality of who I was in the present. In those moments of choice, when my memory of who I had been in the past went head-to-head with my unfolding awareness of the me I was becoming, it took even greater effort for me to stop—to notice, own, and celebrate the positive shifts in my personality, my relationships, the ways I related to life, and the ways I allowed life to relate to me—and then, from that place of awareness, to begin to allow the new me to take the lead in living my own life.

I only later learned that I was not alone in my need to play catch up. The more I talked with my mentees, the more I realized that they too often fell behind in their awareness of their own in-the-moment transformation process. This was not their fault—often, just like I had been when I had stood in their shoes, they were simply too busy doing the hard work of recovery to sit back and notice that it was *working*.

It has been for this reason—for the purposes of allowing them to notice that they *do* have a reemerging sense of who they are as free from the eating disorder's influence—that I have often asked my mentees to complete a deceptively simple, identity-strengthening questionnaire.

So now, in this Workshop, I will ask you to complete this questionnaire right along with them. Like I have told my mentees, each question will ask you to define or describe a facet of your personality or preferences—in a way that is free from the influence of your eating disorder voice. (Because your eating disorder voice, of course, likes to relate everything about you back to your shape, size, or the number you see on a scale!) And if, as some of my mentees have experienced, your eating disorder voice tries to tell you that you can't answer some of these questions, or that it knows the answers better than you do, or that there will be consequences for completing the exercise, then simply tell it this: "I have Shannon's permission to answer each and every question. She has beaten you, and so she outranks you. I am beating you too—watch me beating you even now as I answer each question with my full willingness and Shannon's full permission!"

So, here in part one of this Recovery Workshop, try your hand at the questionnaire and see what you come up with. Make sure you write down each question and your answer in your journal so you can complete part two of the exercise as well. I also highly recommend that you try not to think too much—or at all, if possible—about your answers but rather let them be spontaneous. This is a nifty way to circumvent the eating disorder voice, which will probably try to answer for you regardless of your resolve not to let it. Even better, it is also a great way to hear your heart's answer—and thus the truthful answer—for each question. If you find that you are tempted to blow off answering any of the questions as childish or unimportant, or your eating disorder voice tries to tell you that the questions are unimportant, just ask yourself what part of you is uncomfortable with building an identity separate from your eating disorder, remind your eating disorder of who is in charge, and then try answering the question(s) again.

1. What is your ethnic background (ancestry, parents, grandparents, etc.)?

2. What do you look like (eye color, skin tone, hair color, *no numbers!*)?

3. What are your hobbies/talents?

4. Do you prefer mornings or evenings?

5. Do you prefer the mountains or the ocean?

6. What is your ultimate dream if you could have/be/do anything you wanted?

7. Why do you want to recover?

8. Do you want kids (if you don't already have them)?

9. If you want kids, how many do you want and what gender(s)?

10. Do you already have kids (names, ages, etc.)?

11. Are you married (give details about your wedding day, your husband/wife; if you're not married and would like to someday be, answer what your dreams are of your husband/wife and wedding day)?

12. What kind of music do you like?

13. What is your favorite sport or exercise activity?

14. What is your favorite inspirational saying?

15. What is the best movie you've ever seen and why?

16. What is the best book you've ever read and why?

17. If you could live anywhere in the world (or visit), where would that be and why?

18. If you could meet anyone alive or dead, who would it be and why, and what would you say or ask them?

19. What is your favorite type of food (Italian, Mexican, etc.)?

20. Do you sleep with one pillow or two (or none or more)?

21. Do you prefer group sports or solo sports?

22. Do you prefer cold drinks or hot drinks?

23. What is your dream job or career?

24. Would you ever get a tattoo or piercing?

25. If you have a tattoo or piercing now, where is it located and what is its significance?

26. What is your favorite car?

27. If someone handed you a check for a million dollars, what would you do first?

28. You have a free Friday night—nothing planned. What is your favorite way to spend it?

29. What is your favorite flower?

30. What is your favorite saying or motto?

31. If you could leave a lasting legacy for the next generation, what would it be and why?

Now, you are ready for part two of the exercise. Take some time to read through each of your answers. First, celebrate yourself for answering them all! This is a huge accomplishment—bigger than you might realize at this moment. You have declared freedom from your eating disorder by remembering and clearly writing out a comprehensive set of characteristics that define you and your life—your preferences, hopes, dreams, and choices—all of which have nothing to do with the eating disorder's influence over you in the past or the present, and all of which also speak intently and decisively of a time in the near future when your eating disorder's role in your life will be a distant memory.

Next, read through your answers again, pretending that you are reading about someone else—someone you have been wanting to meet and have been curious about for some time now. Notice how great it feels to focus on a curiosity, a wonder, an interest in who *you* are, rather than what is probably your more usual habit of focusing on anything the eating disorder voice may have told you to focus on. There is a whole person in there—in you—that has just been obscured through your eating disorder's hold over your mind—until now.

The important point to get here is that you are not the eating disorder—rather, you have an eating disorder that is interfering with your sense of who you really are. But not anymore! Through this exercise, you have just proven to yourself comprehensively that you are not your eating disorder—you are *you!*

Be sure to add to and build on this questionnaire each time you have a new insight about any of the questions, or think of a new question about yourself and your life that you are curious to know your own answer to, until you have compiled a complete self-portrait that stands strong and clear of the eating disorder's influence. Creating and maintaining a strong self-identity apart from the eating disorder is a surefire way to set your mind on a firm path toward saving your own life, as you really get to know the new *you*, who has so much to offer, who has so much potential and promise, and who is so worth saving!

Life Celebration Affirmation:

There is a power struggle going on inside you right now—the "old you" (with the help of your eating disorder) and the "new you" are fighting like little children over a favored toy, which in this case is your life. To ease the tension within, it is time to reassure all facets of you—past, present, and future—that they are known, valued, treasured, respected, heard, affirmed, understood, accepted, and loved.

Whenever you feel tempted to believe anything less than the best for yourself and your life, you can affirm these or similar words:

I am both my brightest heights and my darkest depths, and everything in between. I honor the entire vast panorama of my past thoughts, experiences, and actions for all that they have taught me, and I bid them fond farewell now as I move ahead. From this point forward, I choose to see myself from the highest perspective. I deserve it. I have earned it. By my very determination to heal and overcome the deadly effects of the eating disorder within me, I have already proven to myself that I have what it takes to be all that I can be. Now, I choose to live like it by taking the time to really get to know myself—to meet and welcome the new me!

Just Get Over It

Hi Shannon—

Well, I'll be very honest, right now I feel very guilty for writing to you about me and my problems. I hate it! I actually sat here reading this after I was done and almost didn't send it because of how it makes me feel. But I know that I need help, and being that you have been where I am, it makes me feel good that I don't have to try and explain this to you like I do to so many. You get it and understand it, and I know you aren't going to tell me it's something I just need to get over. I wish it was that easy because I would just get over it [the eating disorder] if I could.

Jenna

Dear Jenna—

We were born into a time when there are more ways to sideswipe and stun us into believing there is something wrong with us than at any other time in history.

So if you're not talking about these choices and consequences with someone, someone who cares, someone who knows, then guess what voice you'll be left listening to? The voice of the eating disorder. And this is why, especially right now, the someone you talk to doesn't have to be me, but it has to be someone. No matter who it is, you must have someone you can talk to while you work toward healing and recovery, or you *will not heal*.

Shannon

RECOVERY WORKSHOP

How many times have we all heard, thought we heard, thought to ourselves, yelled at ourselves, been yelled at by others, *"Just get over it!"*

And how many people do you know—can you actually *name*—who have been able to complete, all by themselves, this deceptively, unfairly simple-sounding task?

I, personally, right off the top of my head, cannot think of anyone. Not. One. Single. Person. Spiders, mice, clams, guppies, turtles, antelopes . . . they don't have the problems that we do, because mostly they don't get second chances to learn. If they don't make the right choice the first time, then whatever is just ahead of them on the food chain knows what it is having for lunch.

We are different. We get second chances. And in recovery, later if not sooner and after as many chances as it takes, we will finally learn that, in order to "just get over it" we must go *through* it and humble ourselves to ask for help.

Oh, yes. The dreaded *H* word. As in, "I couldn't do this alone and neither can you." As in, "It helps me as much to help you as it will help you to allow me to help, so please don't make either of us do this alone."

You feel very alone right now—I don't even need to know you personally to know that you feel alone, because I too felt very alone when I was battling my eating disorder—especially in the loneliest years before I met my mentor. Even after I met my mentor, there were days I still felt alone. No one in this world who lives with an eating disorder or who loves someone who lives with an eating disorder can avoid feeling alone. Eating disorders, in order to flourish, require loneliness. They demand it. In fact, they live for and on it, eventually even going so far as to kill their hosts in order to achieve the total isolation they crave. This is why you simply must remember that:

RELATIONSHIPS REPLACE EATING DISORDERS.

In this Workshop, you will commit to inviting three people to partner with you in recovery over the next seven days, remembering all the while that help is a two-way street—no one gives without a need to receive, and no one receives without a corresponding need to give. I will tell you up front that I do know that this is one of—if not *the*—toughest exercise in this entire book. This is why I have saved it for the very last . . . after you have done so much work, and it has become virtually impossible for you to find proof that you "can't" do anything you put your powerful mind to— especially if it is something that will help you to achieve your recovery goals!

Regardless, I do remember how I felt the first time I attempted this assignment, so I can imagine that you too might be feeling dread, fear, even a desire to scale back your recovery goals and hopes to avoid it . . . *don't.* You have come so far, but your eating disorder is a powerful disease, and it is vital not to underestimate it—no matter how much progress you have made. You must find something stronger than the eating disorder to replace it with if you want your recovery to last. The only thing stronger than the eating disorder, that has even more determination to prevail, is your human heart. And when two or three hearts are joined together for a common goal—to make sure that your recovery grows and lasts—well, then your eating disorder simply doesn't stand a chance!

Furthermore, in encouraging you to dive into this final exercise and give it everything you've got, I urge you to remember that each person who *accepts* your invitation to be a part of your support circle will do so with the awareness that they too need to stay connected to courageous people like themselves—courageous people like *you*—in order to live their lives to the fullest. You are not a burden or needy by asking someone else for help and support— rather, you are a *participant* in the human experience of helping, being helped, and then passing it on.

Your three people do not need to be familiar with eating disorders (although it would help if they have some experience in recovery-related issues, if at all possible). They do need to be familiar with you, and to care about you and your well-being and be able to express that care to you in a way that is free from judgment, excessive fear, or the desire to take charge of your recovery process.

You do not need to designate one of these three people as your mentor, although if you already have a mentor, then he or she can be one of your three people.

If you are having trouble explaining to your three people exactly what you need help with, it may be helpful to first brainstorm in your journal a "wish list" of activities they could engage in with you to support you—things that would make a difference in your ability to give your recovery work your full and enthusiastic effort. For instance, maybe you need to know that one of them is "on call" at meal times to answer your phone calls or texts for support while you eat—or even to join you for meals once or twice a week. Maybe you need a ride to/from therapy sessions, support group meetings, or doctor visits. Perhaps you are just beginning your recovery work and you haven't yet told significant family members about your eating disorder, and you need a supportive friend to come with you as you share this news. Maybe you haven't even fully confirmed your fears that you do have an eating disorder as of yet, and you need a friend to come with you to your initial assessment appointment. Maybe you are actively pursuing recovery while caring for your family, and you need someone to babysit, or help with meals or rides for your spouse and dependents while you are at appointments. Maybe you just need to get away and have some fun—and you would enjoy the companionship of someone who knows what you are going through even if you are just watching a movie or taking a walk together. You could also invite any or all of your three people to work with you on the exercises in this book—and perhaps even start with this one.

It is not necessary that each of your three people be made aware of the other two or that you develop any particular sort of structure for the type of support they each and all offer to you. Ultimately, the purpose of this exercise is far simpler and far more profound. As you give yourself permission to be in close relationships with people you care about in whatever way that works for each of you, you enable yourself to move closer to your ultimate goal of replacing your dependence on the eating disorder with the interdependence of real human relationships!

Also remember that those who are not ready or able to participate in any capacity as a supportive partner to you while you recover (which may say more about where they are in their lives than what they think about where you are in yours) will let you know by saying no. Move on without fear, knowing that those who are ready, willing, and able to support you are standing by to let you know this by saying yes.

Finally, before you begin, I can also share with you that, even after I met my mentor, for many years I was still very shy about telling other people I knew that I was in recovery from an eating disorder, let alone asking for their friendship and support during my recovery process. I didn't think they would understand. In hindsight, I realize today that my fear of others not understanding said a lot more about my own lack of understanding of and respect for what I had been through and what I was trying to accomplish by recovering than it did about their actual lack of understanding. I have learned, in the years since I completed the bulk of my recovery work, that the people in my life are usually willing to help and support me—in fact they want to help and support me—but often they don't know how. I have also learned that they are usually as afraid of rejection as I am—in offering their support to me without first being asked, they fear hearing me say "No!"

So, in completing this final assignment, do not let your mind unsettle you with doubt, fear, indecision, or assurances of "certain" rejection. As a matter of fact, you have already accepted yourself by choosing to involve yourself fully in your recovery process, and where there is a little acceptance, even more is sure to follow. So instead, begin by simply considering all avenues where you might find help—family, friends, support communities (on- and off-line), nonprofit and spiritual organizations, recovery centers, medical facilities, campuses and neighborhood associations . . . brainstorm every single place you can think of, and then every single person you can think of, and list the places and names as they come to you. Do not judge or censor your list. Do not allow yourself to assume a yes or a no before you have heard it from that person's own lips.

Next, call, write, e-mail, text, or schedule an in-person visit with each person you have chosen. The purpose of this initial contact will be simply to share a bit about your story and your present need for support (share only as much as you feel comfortable with, which may be different for each person you approach). Then wait for their reply, trusting that the support you are seeking is there and allowing it to come to you in the way that is best for all concerned. If you get stuck in what to say, you might want to consider using the sample letter that follows as a starting point, and then just modifying it with your personal information and for the method of initial contact you select:

Dear [enter name],

I am [calling/writing/e-mailing] to share something important with you—something that is a huge life goal of mine. I haven't shared this with [anyone/many people] but your [friendship/presence in my life] is [precious/a source of inspiration], and I have wanted to tell you about my goal for some time now. I am working toward my recovery from an eating disorder. I have been doing this work for [number of days/months/years] and am finding that having the encouragement of [my community/friends/family] is important as I heal. Sometimes it is helpful for me to talk about my recovery work with people who care about me and can cheerlead for me and encourage me. I was hoping that you might consider being one of those people in my life as I continue my recovery process. I chose you because [share your reason(s) here]. I have some ideas for specific ways I need support [here you can share the work you are doing in this book/attending support group meetings together/phone calls during tough moments/going to dinner together/etc.], and I would also love to learn more from you about where you might be willing and able to be a part of my recovery process.

Thank you for honoring me and my goal by [reading this letter/listening to me] and for considering becoming a part of my support team. I hope you know as you [read/hear this] that you are appreciated and loved!

[insert a preferable closing here],
[your name]

Over the next seven days, the eating disorder's lonely world will shrink as your world expands with the fullness, relief, and joy of real relationships. Surprise yourself and those around you with your courage and determination to go to any lengths to beat your eating disorder at its own game—even going so far as to open the door of your heart to love.

Love is the one force in this universe that can comfort, redirect, and inspire even the most rebellious and negative mind to transform itself into a force that can make an eating disorder stop dead in its tracks, stare, turn, and flee—never to be seen again!

If you want your eating disorder out of your life once and for all, the surest way to accomplish this is to *let love in*.

Life Celebration Affirmation:

You are worth knowing and loving. Your eating disorder will always beg to differ, so ask for a second opinion. And a third ... and as many as you need until you begin to realize that your eating disorder's is the only opinion in your entire supportive circle that does not now, never has, and never will have your best interests at heart—and thus deserves not one single moment more of your time or consideration! You know better now. You do better now. And whenever you are once again tempted to listen to the ghost of starvation-, binges-, or purges-past, you can remind yourself to listen instead to these or similar words reverberating within you:

I am worth knowing and loving. I am worth salvaging and resurrecting. Even in being helped, I cannot help but to offer help in return, and offering help is the very best use of a life. It is a contribution worth surviving and thriving for. It is a gift that keeps on giving, as I join others all around me in managing our common human condition the best way we know how: by leaning on each other for support! I commit to allowing others to help me, and to turning around and offering my help in return. In this way, I further commit to finding and taking my rightful place in this world—one hand stretched out behind me to someone who needs it, all the while grabbing hold of the helping hand stretched out to me. There is no better use of a life, and I am proud to call this life my life. My life is my very own, and I now commence to really live it!

Epilogue:
The Rose Garden

I n closing, I would like to invite you to share one of my favorite contemplations. Imagine that you have a lovely little house where you have lived all of your life. In your backyard there grows a large, riotously beautiful rose garden. In this garden is every color and size and shape and variety of rose. Every morning you are privileged to step outside your back door to watch the sunrise and witness the beauty of the roses waking up to a new day. As far as you know, roses are the only flower you have ever seen. As far as you know, there is no other flower but a rose. And, of course, you think the rose is the most beautiful thing in the whole world.

But then, one day when you wake up and walk outside, you stop dead in your tracks. Your unbelieving eyes are fixed upon a most unexpected and unwelcome sight. Because there, growing up strong and tall, *right in the middle* of your prized rose garden, is a very large, round, sunshine-yellow *daisy*.

What would you do? What *do* you do?

When I ask my middle school girls this question, I receive a colorful (and sometimes violent) medley of answers. Some shout out immediately, "Cut it down!" Others, when I call on them, shake their heads and say they don't know. Usually, one girl will eventually raise her hand and softly utter these words, "I would leave it if I think it is pretty."

And I reply, "Bingo!"

You see, finding, feeling, and experiencing beauty is all up to you. It is *your choice.*

Our eating disorders have taught us to see our beauty through the deliberately distorted lenses of the media-marketing-driven culture we dwell in, and the equally compelling propensity for the disease that dwells within us. However, that does not mean we have to *stay* in that uncomfortable, unhappy place, trying to wedge our brilliant unique beauty into the sharp-edged little cookie-cutter mold that fits none of us well.

Some of my best days have been the days when I could begin to see something beautiful in not only myself but in absolutely every other person I met as well. Believe it or not, this is a learned art. Like happiness or optimism, perceiving beauty is a deliberate choice and a very real ability we can develop. Those of us who learn it young usually have been privileged to have had parents, guardians, or caretakers who first mastered the lesson themselves, and then passed its secret on to us. The rest of us are left to learn it the hard way, on our own, and some of us are forced to learn it in the hardest way of all, by first enduring the ravages of an eating disorder.

So now I will ask you again. What would *you* do? What would you do with that big, bright, round, sunshine-yellow daisy, brazenly strutting its stuff smack-dab in the middle of your carefully cultivated roses-only garden?

Say you cut it down. Just say you, in a moment of blind fury, panic, indignation, insecurity, indecision, or fear, grab the garden shears and snap it off at its stalk. Feeling instantly self-satisfied and relieved, you saunter back indoors. Problem solved. A few moments later, your front doorbell unexpectedly rings. "Who could it be?" you wonder to yourself. You look through the peephole and see your brand-new next-door neighbor standing there, waiting to introduce herself. When you open the door, your neighbor smiles cheerily and invites you over for a quick cup of introductory coffee and some homemade cinnamon rolls. "Yum!" you think (because of course you are living completely free from your eating disorder by now, and cinnamon rolls are your favorite!)

Your friendly neighbor hands you a cup of steaming hot coffee and a fresh-from-the-oven cinnamon roll, and invites you out into the backyard to sit in a pair of comfy garden chairs and enjoy the chill morning.

Just as you walk out the back door into the morning sunshine, what do your amazed eyes behold but a large, riotously enthusiastic *daisy* garden spanning the entire length of your neighbor's backyard! Daisies in all sizes, shapes, and colors; daisies of every variety ... everywhere you look you see nothing but *daisies, daisies, daisies*. Your neighbor begins to tell you about each daisy, their breed and value, where each one came from and what they represent.

Suddenly, it becomes clear to you just where that cheery renegade in your garden might have come from.

And suffice it to say that, depending on the choice you made earlier to cut it down or not, you might return home with a lot to think about.

I will repeat it one more time, this one simple truth.

Finding, feeling, and experiencing beauty is all up to you.

It is your choice. It is my choice. It is our choice. It is our *right*—to find, feel, and experience the unique beauty we see displayed in each other and in ourselves. No one can take that right and that experience away from us—no one can, or will, *unless we ourselves give it away.*

So, now, *take back* your beauty. Take back the beauty in your own skin, the beauty in your own life, the beauty in the lives all around you. Take back the vision to see beauty in all of the people and places where you previously allowed yourself none. Take back your right to claim beauty in the infinite, unique variety so freely available to your eyes, ears, mind, body, heart, spirit. Take back your right to define what beauty is to you, how it speaks, walks, talks, breathes, forms, creates, and lives. Take back your right to accept and experience this wondrous gift for yourself, and then reclaim your right to turn around and share the moments of beauty in your life with us all.

I said it once when we first began this journey together. I will say it again as we walk forward together now, side by side, into the unrepeatable beauty of recovered life . . . do we, do any of us, ever really realize . . .

You are the only you who ever was, is, or ever will be.
And I am the only me.

Sometimes I feel like I have more to say to myself—to you here in these pages, to everyone I meet—but I just can't find the words. So for now, let me just say—

TRUST. HOPE. FAITH. LOVE. LIVE. **TRIUMPH.** BELIEVE.

Warmly and with *hope,*

Shannon

Mentoring 101

The process of mentoring offers mentors and mentees alike the chance to engage in a mutually empowering partnership to facilitate and strengthen recovery. The following guidelines can assist you in beginning, building, and maintaining a mentoring bond that can become an enduring source of joy and inspiration throughout your recovery journey.

You can find more information about mentoring, and learn about opportunities to participate in the mentoring process, by visiting www.key-to-life.com.

What you make of your life is up to you. You have all the resources you need. What you do with them is up to you. The choice is yours.

—Rules for Being Human, *author unknown*

Guidelines for Mentors

1. **Refrain** from volunteering to serve as a mentor until you are in strong recovery (at least one year largely free from symptoms of disordered eating and all other related unhealthy behaviors and coping patterns).

2. **Before beginning to serve as a mentor,** be clear and honest with yourself about your motivations for doing so. Do not rush yourself through your own recovery because you wish to help others!

3. **The wise and effective mentor will first and always be a mentee as well.** Find your balance between giving out of the fullness of what you have learned and earned through your own recovery, and yet always continuing to receive centering guidance and instruction from those ahead of you on the recovery path.

4. **Be very clear** with your mentee(s) before beginning a mentoring relationship about the time commitment you can make. If you are only available via e-mail or phone, say so. If you are only available on certain days, say so. Then take care to be consistent with the availability you have offered to your mentee(s) and to quickly and clearly communicate any changes to your availability that may arise.

5. **Safeguard your own recovery** and **do not take on more than you can handle!** If the mentor-mentee relationship develops into a partnership that requires more time

and/or energy than you are able to offer, redirect your mentee(s) to find a more appropriate match and/or additional support resources.

6. **Be willing to halt or end the relationship** if at any time it appears that your mentee is no longer willing to actively work toward recovery, or if the relationship itself becomes an impediment or a detriment to the mentee's progress in recovery or to your own continued strong recovery.

7. **Require** all mentee(s) who are minors to obtain parent or legal guardian permission before entering into a mentoring relationship.

8. **Do not attempt** to supersede or replace other treatment options or team members—seek to be a complement to any structure already in place and encourage your mentee(s) to build a network that includes any and all options that are needed/available (can include treatment team members, such as a medical doctor, psychiatrist, therapist, dietician/nutritionist, and also local community organizations, support groups, family members, and friends).

9. **Use extreme caution** when making recommendations outside of any recovery-related life experience, training, or expertise you may have. Partner with other treatment professionals and/or guide your mentee(s) to seek additional assistance from qualified medical practitioners in selecting other support team members.

10. **Clearly communicate** to mentee(s) that any insight/ feedback you offer as a mentor is *not* meant to replace the advice and care of a medical professional.

11. **Remember the mentor-mentee relationship is voluntary** and that it is the mentee's job to make good use of the opportunity. You may even consider asking your mentee to sign an agreement attesting to his or her awareness and acceptance of what you have to offer in terms of your time and input, and what you expect in exchange in terms of regular communication and effort toward meeting stated recovery goals. This will serve to keep you from becoming overloaded as a mentor and will assist potential mentees in assessing whether they are truly ready, willing, and able to enter into a mentoring relationship.

12. **Focus on troubleshooting** for daily living and recovery-related issues *as they arise*. Per #11 above, allow your mentee to come to you with specific requests for whatever they need support with, and then you can respond accordingly with compassion and creative ideas for new coping skills. If your mentee seems shy about asking for help, you might consider asking, "What are you struggling with today/this week?" However, do not attempt to drive or lead your mentee in his or her recovery work. Your role as a mentor is always *re*active to your mentee's requests for support and demonstrated willingness to do the hard work of recovery.

13. **Share your personal story only as one example.** Remember that each person's story is unique.

14. **Strive above all** to awaken the wise and confident healer within your mentee(s).

15. **Be committed,** available, open and honest, patient, kind, and willing to be wrong. Remember that mentoring is a very unique relationship, and like any successful partnership, there must be a certain "chemistry" that indicates there is a good match. Do not be discouraged if the relationship feels a bit tentative or awkward at first as you get to know one another. Do not be afraid to release your mentee or yourself from a partnership that does not seem to be bearing fruit or to hang on when progress is slow but visible.

16. **Remember what it was like** for you during your own recovery and adjust recommendations/expectations accordingly. Patience here can work miracles.

17. **Remember that the #1 healer** is unconditional love.

18. **Faithful, consistent, positive feedback** is key.

19. **Depersonalize the process.** Focus on achieving desired results more than on adoption of specific suggestions.

20. **In the presence of triggers, proceed with caution.** Instead of becoming overly involved in discussions of numbers, weight, and so on, pinpoint what these topics may represent and how to address those underlying issues successfully.

21. **Avoid** any attempt to coerce mentee(s) into wanting to heal or doing the work. Instead, emphasize the benefits of recovery as you have experienced them.

22. **Be ready** to seek additional support or to notify those who are authorized to act on your mentee's behalf if the situation appears life-threatening. If at any point you begin to perceive that your mentee needs more support than you are qualified to offer, do not hesitate to communicate that clearly and, if the option exists, refer him or her to a higher level of care. Your job as a mentor is not to play the hero. As we know, eating disorders are dangerous, unpredictable diseases, and they are also masters of disguise. Let your mentee know up front that your ability to keep confidentiality extends only so far as you are not aware that she is becoming a danger to herself or others. In cases where it is clear that your mentee needs more comprehensive support and you do not know who to contact on her behalf, you may find that you are forced to make the heart-wrenching decision to walk away, knowing there is nothing you can do to help further at this moment in time. But ultimately, just like it was for you when you were healing, it is up to your mentee(s) to choose recovery actively by doing the work, however difficult it may become. While this may not provide much solace in the moment, keeping this overarching awareness at all times during the mentoring process assists you in serving as a responsible mentor.

Guidelines for Mentees

1. **Screen your mentor carefully.** Accept only a mentor who has demonstrated sustained remission from disordered eating and all other related unhealthy behaviors and coping patterns for at least twelve consecutive months.

2. **Seek complementary recovery experiences.** While it is not necessarily essential that your mentor has achieved recovery from the exact same issue you are struggling with (he or she could be in recovery for alcoholism, substance abuse, codependency, or other related areas), your mentor should at a minimum have firsthand experience of going through the recovery process itself with demonstrated success as per #1 above.

3. **Be clear about your readiness and motivations for seeking mentoring.** If you can state verbally and in writing with 100 percent certainty that you are ready, willing, and able (i.e., nutritional/weight stabilization has been achieved and maintained for at least one month) to work toward your own recovery, then you know that you are ready to seek a mentor.

4. **Trust your gut.** Mentoring is a unique relationship, and it may take a couple of tries to find the right "fit" for your needs.

5. **If you are a minor,** obtain parent or legal guardian permission before seeking a mentor or accepting an offer to be mentored.

6. **Do not attempt** to use the advice or insight of your mentor to replace the advice and care of a qualified medical professional. Instead, integrate your mentor into any existing support network you already have and be prepared to expand your network whenever necessary to address all of your recovery needs.

7. **Be open and honest** with any existing treatment team about the inclusion of your mentor and with your mentor about other members of your treatment team.

8. **Communicate clearly** with your mentor about what you are hoping to obtain out of a mentoring relationship.

9. **Follow the guidelines** your mentor provides for maintaining regular contact.

10. **Be proactive.** Use the support and experience of your mentor whenever you feel the need.

11. **Practice the H.O.W. of recovery.** Be honest, open, and willing to explore new ways of responding to life's challenges, try on new ideas for size, and put into practice suggestions before accepting or rejecting their validity.

12. **Under no circumstances** should you adopt any suggestion or idea that holds the potential to have a negative impact on your recovery goals, *even if* it has worked well for someone else in their recovery! For instance, if you know that something is triggering to you, like a certain form of exercise or reading certain types of books, do not be afraid to say no to suggestions from your mentor to use those

things for support. Even if your mentor and others have found them helpful, you need to work with your mentor to discover your own avenues for support that are healthy and helpful to you.

13. **Focus on daily troubleshooting** to build skills to use in place of your eating disorder in stressful situations. Remember that, while your mentor may not have the qualifications or expertise to advise you in every area of your recovery, he or she has gone all the way through the day-to-day process of recovering. Do not judge issues that arise in your recovery as small or large, or as worthy or unworthy of your mentor's attention. When you run into difficulty in your day-to-day recovery work and with using your new coping skills, *ask* your mentor for support.

14. **Do not be too concerned** if your mentor's personal story varies from your own. Focus more on the underlying coping skills that aided your mentor in his or her recovery process and how you might apply them in your own life as well.

15. **Do not place the responsibility for your recovery** on your mentor or on any other treatment team member—it is you who will benefit the most from your own recovery.

16. **Seek progress over perfection.** Even if your mentor can now clearly and quickly articulate potential solutions to issues you are facing, remember that your mentor was once standing in your shoes. It takes time for *everyone* to

achieve lasting recovery! You are no exception, and anything worth having is worth waiting and working for—no matter how long it takes.

17. **Set your own pace for your recovery.** Do not allow anyone to push you into situations or experiences for which you feel inadequately prepared.

18. **Let love be your guide.** If you feel consistent, foundational love and support from your mentor, regardless of any temporary differences of opinion, fears, or resistances that may arise, then that is a good indication that the relationship is still productive and worth continuing.

A "Model" Mentoring Relationship

So how exactly *does* a mentoring relationship work?

While it is not possible to give a blanket answer, for the simple reason that each mentoring relationship should, must, and will be unique to its participants' needs and preferences, there are some common denominators that can help in structuring a mentoring relationship that invites a higher potential for success.

To outline such a possible structure, and illustrate the use of many of the guidelines listed above, I would like to share the stories of how the mentoring relationship began and progressed for me with two of the courageous women you have now met through these pages—Nadia and Michelle.

Nadia

Nadia, an adult woman in recovery from anorexia and bulimia, heard me speak at her treatment facility. When Nadia returned home, she e-mailed me to share that she was finding coming home to be a rough process. I replied with a message of support and an offer to keep in touch. Nadia began e-mailing every week or so with questions about the recovery process. I replied as soon as I was able. Sometimes I was able to reply that very same day, and sometimes it would take me a few days or a week to respond. I was always clear with Nadia by saying, "I welcome your questions, and please know that I will respond just as soon as I possibly can. If it takes me a few days, please be patient." Nadia saw her therapist on a weekly basis and was also working actively with a dietician. Over the years, as Nadia's recovery strengthened and she made progress, she learned to take charge of her own recovery process. Sometimes she would e-mail me with questions or concerns, and other times she would share joys and triumphs. She became closer with her family and began working part-time again. In time, I only heard from Nadia occasionally to say "Hi." She was living again, and her eating disorder had become a minor player in her very full, real life!

Michelle

Michelle, a high school student in recovery from anorexia, met me through the *Key to Life* forum on MySpace, which led to my visit to her town during a National Eating Disorders Awareness

Week (NEDA) event. Her family met me and gave permission for Michelle to stay in touch with me about her recovery. Michelle began e-mailing me regularly during the summer before her freshman year of college. She was excited but nervous at the big change life had in store for her and wanted support and encouragement during the transition. During her freshman year of college, Michelle began to struggle greatly with her eating disorder. She e-mailed me every few weeks between exams to ask for support. Michelle had access to on-campus counseling and I encouraged her to take full advantage of support closer to home and to continue to e-mail me as well. I supported Michelle in reaching out for help from her roommates, treatment team, campus counseling center staff, family members, and friends, including her boyfriend. As she works toward strengthening her recovery, Michelle continues to e-mail me regularly for support and insight into how to approach recovery stumbling blocks and make the most of her choice to live a recovered life.

The Hidden Power of Mentoring

Remembering back to my very first experiences of mentoring others, I recall feeling daunted, doubtful, and a little scared as I considered becoming a mentor to someone else for the very first time. Fresh from my own recovery experiences of being mentored, self-esteem intact but still just the tiniest bit fragile, I remember wondering how I could know whether I was capable of doing good in someone else's life.

This is how I discovered the *hidden power of mentoring*. Because it was only *after* I accepted the honor and the challenge of taking on my first mentee that I realized I already knew how. Like choosing recovery for the first time, I had to simply *feel the fear and do it anyway*.

You will know that you know how to be someone's mentor— when you do it. This is because you awaken your own full awareness of just how far you have come and all that you have first received only when you begin to share it with someone else. A good friend of mine who also serves as a mentor has this to say about her experiences of mentoring others: "I encourage anybody who is now recovering from eating disorders to consider the great and life-enhancing gift of giving back. Many, many struggling people would benefit enormously from having a mentor. Here is an opportunity to enhance your own recovery and transform your pain and struggles into a gift of wisdom and empathy."

I couldn't have said it any better myself.

If you want to become completely confident in your own recovery, if you want to feel your feet firmly planted on the ground of recovered life, if you long to own what you have and know that it is yours for life, then *pay it forward*. You will never truly know how high you can fly until you begin to teach someone else who has watched you in flight and longs to learn.

Ultimately, whether our current role is as a mentee or as a mentor, recovery is best accomplished, and longest lasting, when we achieve it *together*.

In the Beginning . . .

In mentoring, as in recovery and in life, the very best place to begin is . . . you guessed it—at the beginning!

You have nothing to lose by reaching out and absolutely everything to gain. If at first you do not find a mentor, or a perfect match for your mentoring needs, *try again*. I owe my life to my mentors, and my mentors owe their lives to their mentors. And on it goes.

On either side of the recovery coin, your life is so worth saving and so worth sharing. Do not doubt. *Know*. If you are considering seeking a mentor, know that we are out there, waiting to meet and support you—and that we are grateful for your commitment to recovery. If you are considering becoming a mentor, know that you are deeply needed, valued, and cherished—and that we are grateful for your willingness to serve.

Mentoring is one of life's true wonders, and it is a lifelong learning process. I learn something new every single day. If you have questions about the mentoring process, and/or wish to share your own experiences with mentoring, I would love to hear from you and will respond to all questions in the order received through the *Key to Life* website. You can write to me at book@key-to-life.com.

Your answers lie inside you. The answers to life's questions lie inside you. All you need to do is look, listen, and trust.

—Rules for Being Human, *author unknown*

About *Key to Life* and *Mentor*CONNECT

Shannon founded *Key to Life: unlocking the door to hope* when she first began serving as a mentor in 2004. Whether working one-on-one as a mentor or presenting the messages of *Key to Life* to a larger audience, her focus has always been simple: To "unlock the door to hope" for those who suffer from eating and related disorders by activating their awareness that they do have something worth fighting and recovering for—their "key to life." Today, *Key to Life* continues to offer a wide variety of exciting and uplifting events, workshops, concerts, products, and services that foster awareness, education, intervention, and prevention of eating and related disorders for students, families, educators, clinicians, and whole communities. You can learn more about how you can schedule or attend a *Key to Life* event and access supportive recovery resources by visiting www.key-to-life.com.

Founded by Shannon and led by a team of four experts in the recovery field, *Mentor*CONNECT is an exciting new *Key to Life* community created to offer the power of mentoring to YOU and to those you care about who need support during the recovery process. Whether you wish to serve as a mentor or you are seeking a mentor, you will discover that *Mentor*CONNECT is a place where relationships really *can* and *do* replace eating disorders. This is why, for each *Beating ANA* reader, Shannon is offering you a **FREE TRIAL** membership in *Mentor*CONNECT! Simply visit www.key-to-life.com and click on the "MentorCONNECT" menu bar to get started.

Shannon looks forward to welcoming you to *Mentor*CONNECT very soon!

key to LIFE

unlocking the door to hope

*Mentor*CONNECT

Relationships Replace Eating Disorders

Additional Resources

The *Key to Life* website has a comprehensive list of my favorite books, movies, websites, blogs, current research results, and supportive resources: www.key-to-life.com.

The *Key to Life* website also maintains a current list of support communities I personally participate in, either as a moderator, contributor, or columnist. Visit www.key-to-life.com to learn more.

In addition, if you have found a particular book, movie, website, blog, or support community helpful to your own recovery, please be sure to send it my way: book@key-to-life.com.

Websites

Alcoholics Anonymous and the Twelve Steps: www.aa.org.

Eating Disorders Anonymous: www.eatingdisordersanonymous.org.

Overeaters Anonymous: www.oa.org.

About the Author

Shannon **Cutts** is a compassionate advocate of our right to feel good about ourselves, our bodies, and our lives. As a popular speaker, writer, and award-winning songwriter, she travels year-round, sharing her powerful message that *yes,* recovery from eating disorders *is* possible! After recovering from her own fifteen-year battle with anorexia and bulimia, Shannon founded *Key to Life: unlocking the door to hope,* an organization that offers events, workshops, concerts, products, and services to facilitate eating and related disorders, and *Mentor*CONNECT, a community where mentors and mentees can connect to experience the power of mentoring. Shannon is also the coeditor of *The Book & CD of Companionship for Women Struggling with Eating Disorders, Vol. II* (You Are Not Alone Eating Disorder Society, 2009). *Beating Ana* is her first book.

For more about Shannon, her work, and her availability for speaking and concert engagements, please visit her at www. key-to-life.com.